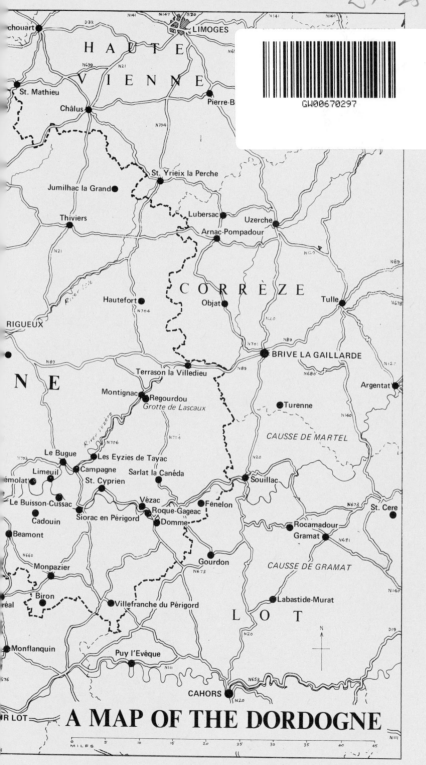

A MAP OF THE DORDOGNE

0   MILES   5   10   15   20   25   30   35   40   45

History, People and Places

in

THE DORDOGNE

The chateau at Bannes

History, People and Places

in

THE DORDOGNE

NEIL LANDS

SPURBOOKS LIMITED

Published by

SPURBOOKS LIMITED
6 Parade Court
Bourne End
Bucks

© **NEIL LANDS** 1975

I.S.B.N. 0 902875 94 9

Made and printed in Great Britain by
The Garden City Press Limited
Letchworth, Hertfordshire SG6 1JS

ACKNOWLEDGEMENTS

The Author and Publishers would like to thank the following people for their assistance in the preparation of this book:
Mrs Pauline Hallam of the French Government Tourist Office in London; the Châtelaines of Chalûs and Biron in the Dordogne; Miss Patricia Dollery; Mrs. Estelle Huxley; and Mr. Terry Brown for help with the maps.

Contents

Illustrations

9

CHAPTER I

An Introduction

The Dordogne is a river in France. It rises in the Auvergne, near Mont Doré, and flows south and west for some 300 miles to marry briefly with the Garonne, at the start of the Gironde estuary above Bordeaux, and so flows at last into the Atlantic. The Dordogne is one of the longest rivers in France and among the most picturesque, flowing as it does through an immense variety of unspoilt country, constantly changing in nature, speed, and direction, in a quest for the open sea.

The Dordogne is also a 'department' of France, named, as so many departments are, from the principal local river, and forms part of the country of Périgord, which lies east of the Atlantic coastline around Bordeaux. Most of the Dordogne lies to the north of the river, and the Department is shaped like a rough diamond, with the four corners reaching out towards Bordeaux in the west, Brive in the east, Montauban in the south, and towards Limoges in the north. Périgueux, the capital of the Dordogne today and once the capital of Périgord, lies roughly in the centre of the Dordogne, some 300 miles south of Paris and 500 miles from the channel coast at Calais.

One can see, therefore, that once in the Dordogne, one is getting towards the South of France, that Provence is not far away, and the climate reflects the sunnier, milder aspects of Southern France, rather than the bleaker outlook of Normandy and the Pas de Calais, two climates more familiar to the English visitor, and the passing traveller.

Not that the inhabitants of Périgord look on themselves as Southerners. They are, if anything, Gascons, or for preference, simply themselves. Nevertheless one can be oneself, and still be glad to live in a place blessed with good weather. The climate of the Dordogne is mild and temperate, tending to become very warm

The Dordogne at Bourdeilles

indeed in the summer, when the heat, on becoming oppressive, is broken by spectacular hail and thunder storms. In the winter snow lies on Mont Doré and the high peaks, and can so lie until early spring, when a good fire is needed for the nights are chill. In the main, though, the area enjoys a fine climate that people from the colder north rightly envy and enjoy.

Snow on the hills might mislead the reader into visualising the Dordogne as a mountainous region. It certainly seems so, with roads winding down the sides of sheer drops, and wooded hills reaching up to the broad plateaux. This is certainly the impression, but mountainous is hardly the word for it. The tallest peak hereabouts is only 1,500 feet high, and while areas around the Massif Central and in the Auvergne are certainly higher, they lie somewhat outside the scope of this book.

This book is about the Dordogne, the Department of the

Dordogne, and only incidentally about the river. It is the Department that people mean when they talk of a holiday or a home 'in the Dordogne', and there is enough history, colour, scenery and interest in that star-shaped country to keep one occupied for a long time, let alone for a holiday. Not that I intend to be a purist about it. In this book little stabs are made across the border, if anything of great interest lies within reach. The boundary of the Department is a control, not a minefield, and we shall cross it if we feel like it.

Now, since we are in some respects going on a journey together, with me, the writer, in the driving seat, it might be as well to list some of my likes and dislikes, since they are the things which you will discover on our journey, while others, equally interesting no doubt, but not to me, will be left out. Let me tell you a little story to illustrate the point.

I was in Moscow once, trailing gloomily around the Kremlin behind the Intourist guide, who spiked every object with some not-so-subtle propaganda, when I saw, on their own, a pair of elderly English tourists. Warmly clad and sensibly shod, they moved doggedly from place to place, stopping at each point of interest. She would identify it on the map, after which he, in a boring monotone, read all the relevant facts from a typescript. Then, having gazed absorbed for some three seconds, they moved on to the next spot, where the process was repeated. It was a terrifying sight and enough to put one off travel for life. Still, it takes all sorts to make a world and, at least, I don't suppose they missed much. But their method is not mine, so be warned. I like to enjoy myself in a less intense fashion.

I like good inns, better food, fine wines, breath-taking scenery, rivers and pools, the occasional waterfall, markets, discreet restaurants, soft sunsets, and peace and quiet. History for me stopped about 1800; politics are of no great concern. My boredom threshold for museums, churches and excessive amounts of the same architecture is very low indeed.

People, on the other hand, living or dead, are a constant source of interest. So there is a lot about people, history, castles, food, wine, where to go, and even a little about architecture, and if these interests coincide with yours then please read on.

I first visited the Dordogne in the middle sixties, on my way south

13

to Spain. Thousands of British tourists must do the same every year, for the roads are full of GB plated cars and caravans, forging south, forming convoys, fiendishly difficult to pass in a left-hand drive car, as they wind slowly over the hills towards the Spanish frontier. Perhaps, like myself, a proportion of these people, in what brief glances they could spare from watching the car in front, became aware that this was a beautiful part of the world they were transversing, and resolved to come back some time. Some must indeed do so, for in the last ten years the Dordogne has become increasingly popular, not only as a holiday area, but also as a place to live. Many British people now have homes in the valleys around the Department, and they or their friends rush south, at the slightest opportunity, to the peaceful woods of the Dordogne. It must be a labour of love to do so, for the Dordogne is not that easy to get to. It is, as we have noted, about 500 miles south of Calais, which is a steady two days' drive if one is not used to driving and wishes to arrive reasonably fresh. One can of course fly to Bordeaux, and hire a car, or cross to Cherbourg and drive down from there, across Normandy and part of Brittany. However you do it, you need a car, and if the distance is not inconsiderable for the British visitor, it is part of the price he will be willing to pay for the relatively unspoilt country and relatively unavaricious people he will meet when he gets there.

The history of France, that vast, mixed, and cultural country of which the Dordogne forms a part, goes back, in direct line, to prehistoric man. The Dordogne provides us with such links, for Cro-Magnon man, one of our earlier ancestors, lived in the valley of the Vézère, while the painted caves at Lascaux, in Dordogne, are famous all over the world as a living example of prehistoric art, dating from some 30,000 years ago.

History, that is, recorded, written history, for this part of the world may be said to begin when Julius Caesar invaded Gaul, and after various campaigns defeated the Gallic chieftain Vercingetorix, at Alesia in 52 BC. Alesia lies in the Côte d'Or, the wine district, to the east of the Dordogne, around Beaune. Roman rule was then applied to the new province of Gaul, and the pattern of development, the creation of towns, roads, and trade, with the introduction of Roman law, spread across the land, and lasted for centuries. As happened elsewhere in the Roman Empire, the customs of the

conquerors were willingly adopted by the nobility among the con-
quered, who largely administered the province to their own commercial advantage, and in many cases became Romanised to the
point of taking on Roman citizenship. Gaul, however, was too large
and diverse ever to be totally assimilated, and parts of the country,
notably the Massif Central where the Dordogne rises, never became
fully Romanised. The tide of Roman culture flowed round this
island of reaction and the main centres of Roman life were on the
coast. Thus we had the *Provincia Romana*, which is now modern
Provence, where, at Nîmes, for example, the Maison Carée and the
Pont du Gard are the finest examples anywhere of the splendour
that was Rome. In the Dordogne, Roman influence is less apparent
for Roman remains are few, but they gave the region as a whole a
name that would endure. They called that region of Gaul, the Land
of Waters, or Acquitania.

The Romans brought Christianity to Gaul, and by the beginning
of the fourth century AD, the new religion was tolerated, and
Christian colonies were springing up everywhere. Among these early
Christians was St. Martin of Tours, one of France's most popular
saints, and more relevant to our subject, St. Hilary of Poitiers. Rome,
however, was now in decline and the legions, those bulwarks of her
imperial power, were going home. In the third century, Franks from
the north and Alemans from across the Rhine invaded Gaul, and
although they were driven off, the threat of further invasion continued to grow, until in the fifth century the Visigoths, no plundering army but settlers, occupied Acquitania, and spread south into
Provence. Their settlement and the final disintegration of Roman
Gaul were hardly established when the Teutonic Franks, under
Clovis, moved south to dominate the country and establish their
rule.

Clovis became a Christian in 496, and, as a Christian King
established the *regnum Francorum*, the kingdom of the Franks,
and the Merovingian dynasty, which collapsed on his death in
AD 551. For the next 200 years what is now France was a land of
petty, squabbling kingdoms, largely Christian in worship, but with
little unity outside religion.

As so often happens, it took an outside threat to unite the
country, and this arrived in the eighth century, when Saracens from
Spain advanced across Acquitania to be defeated by Charles Martel,

at Poitiers, in 732. Charles Martel's grandson united all the Christian kingdoms of the west into the Holy Roman Empire, and called himself Charlemagne.

Charlemagne ruled the Franks from AD 742 until his death in AD 814, and as with Clovis the empire died with him. Fresh barbarian invasions followed, notably that of the Northmen, who established themselves in Normandy.

The descendants of Charlemagne ceased to rule the Franks by descent in 887, when the monarchy became elective. In 987 the Franks elected Hugh Capet as their king, and his house ruled them, and much of France, until 1328, when the House of Valois came to the throne.

The Hundred Years War, which is referred to constantly in the histories of the Dordogne, is only a part of a much longer conflict, and covers the period from Crécy in 1345, which re-established the English as a power in France, and their defeat at Castillion in 1453, which led to their final expulsion. In fact the war lasted for over 300 years, and the tale is full of fascinating complexities.

The French King can hardly have been pleased when William of Normandy won the crown of England in 1066, and become King by right of conquest, owing nothing of this creation to the King of the French except for his homage as Duke of Normandy. There was perhaps some slight advantage to the French in that it moved the restless Norman court from Caen to London, a good deal further away.

However, barely a century later, when the then Henry Plantagenet, Count of Anjou, became not only master of the hereditary Angevin lands, but also King of England, Duke of Normandy, *and* in right of his wife, Duke of Aquitaine, then the French King had a restless vassal who was, in all but name, an emperor, much mightier in economic power and military force than his overlord.

Luckily for the French, the Angevins had within them the seeds of their own ruin, and Henry II's great empire dwindled rapidly after his death, until in the early thirteenth century John was driven from the last Angevin stronghold in Normandy.

Some years later Louis IX, St. Louis, gave back most of the Plantagenet lands to Henry III. In the fourteenth century the French

16

The Dordogne Valley from Montbazillac

had problems for Philip V had only a daughter, who was forbidden by Salic law from inheriting the throne.

Edward III of England claimed the title, but the French chose Philip VI, of Valois, at which Edward promptly invaded, and the Hundred Years War began.

The Dordogne, which had suffered much during the Hundred Years War, enjoyed a respite of no more than another 100 years before the Wars of Religion broke out in France, and the south again became a divided land, ravaged by the opposing factions. The Wars of Religion arose from the spread of the Protestant faith, which seemed to take particular hold in the south, and Henry Bourbon, King of Navarre although born a Catholic, had to turn Huguenot to keep his kingdom of Navarre. Unfortunately he was also heir to the throne of France, but to possess *that* seat he would need to be a Catholic, which would destroy his support in Navarre.

17

While the last Valois kings ruled, religious war spluttered all over France, with bloody massacres, like that of St. Bartholomew's, inflaming the situation. The Dordogne was the great base for the Huguenots, and their captains fought many battles in the land we shall visit.

This is potted history, and a sketchy background to our story, yet it has to be told and understood if the peculiar history of Aquitaine and the people and places of the Dordogne are to be enjoyed in all their fascinating complexity. We shall return to this subject again and again in this book, and the reader should at this point realise that, for much of French history, the King of the French (Rex Francorum) was very far from being the King of France.

Hugh Capet ruled directly only a small area around Paris, generally called the Ile de France, and parts of the north-east. His theoretical power, in the form of people who owed him allegiance, far exceeded his economic or military power. He was, at best, *primus inter pares*, and while his feudal power was great, it was equalled or exceeded by men who were, theoretically, his vassals.

This said, it should not be imagined that the King of the French was ignored by his countrymen. Feudal bonds were no less real for being lightly worn, and the feudal lord would always try and keep his policies broadly in line with those of his sovereign. Unless, of course, it suited him not to.

This, then, was the situation that prevailed with Hugh Capet in 987, and although his descendants pursued a policy of continuous expansion within France, to bring more and more of it under their direct control, it was not until the time of Louis IX, St. Louis, in the early thirteenth century that the major dukedoms and baronies of France were held by feudal right, and at the pleasure of the King, who expected homage from his vassals, and their support in war.

This did not end the problem of rebellions which went on until the seventeenth century, but it formed a major part in making the King of the French into the King of France.

Within this broad framework, let us look at Acquitania, or, as we should now call it, Aquitaine, within the borders of which the Dordogne lies.

During the reign of the Capets, the River Loire divided France

Effigy of Eleanor of Aquitaine

into two very different countries. In the sunlit, tumultuous south, romance and chivalry blossomed in a way quite different from the bluff manners of the north. Even the languages differed, the French 'yes', for example, being pronounced *oui*, north of the Loire, and *oc* south of it, which gave to the south the name of Languedoc. Languedoc presented posterity with the idea of romantic love, which has caused considerable problems to the world ever since. They can hardly be blamed though, for their country was, and is, a romantic place to live in.

In this region Latin was the courtly tongue, and the *langue d'oc* the local patois. Educated men from north of the Loire could understand the *langue d'oc*, but few could speak it.

Within Languedoc lay Aquitaine, one of the two great feudal dukedoms of the south, the other being Toulouse. Aquitaine comprised the counties of Poitou and Gascony, and debated with

19

Toulouse the lordship of Périgord and the Auvergne. The Duke of Aquitaine and the Count of Toulouse were as powerful as their overlord the King, and frequently at war with him, and with each other.

The people of Aquitaine were loyal if turbulent subjects of their Duke, fiercely independent, believing then, as now, that no good could ever come of a ruler from north of the Loire. It was something of a shock, therefore, when their good Duke William IX died on pilgrimage in 1137 and his inheritance fell to his daughter, Eleanor, who was betrothed to the French King Louis VII, whom she then married. The Salic law, which barred women from the throne, only affected the royal inheritance. Eleanor was a fabulously wealthy heiress, apart from being very beautiful, and on their marriage Louis added her lands to his own.

The marriage, however, was not successful. Eleanor was too wilful for her husband, and he bored her to death. Worse, their only child was a daughter, barred by Salic law from the French throne. When she accompanied Louis on the Second Crusade, in 1147, her determination to enjoy herself got the King's army into at least one Saracen ambush, and, during their stay in Antioch, there were some rumours that Eleanor was having an affair with her uncle the reigning Prince of Antioch, Raymond of Aquitaine. By now relations between the King and his wife were at breaking point, and it was common knowledge that they no longer shared the same bed. This, clearly, was no way to provide France with an heir, and on their way home through Italy in 1149, the Pope himself took a hand in the matter, tucking up husband and wife in the same bed, and having given his blessing, left them to get on with it.

The result of this, unfortunately, was yet another daughter, and once again the marriage went into a decline. In 1151 Louis sued for divorce, on the grounds of consanguinity. He could have charged the Queen with adultery, which would have led to her death, but Louis, if dull, was an honourable man, and there was no real proof against the Queen. He even returned to Eleanor her dowry, the Duchy of Aquitaine, a feat of constraint that would have been impossible for most other kings, and in 1152 Eleanor was free. She had, however, to find another husband quickly, to lead her troops and defend her inheritance, so she offered herself to Henry Fitz-Empress, Count of Anjou and Duke of Normandy, who accepted the offer with alacrity; thus came to Aquitaine the most energetic of medieval rulers, who would have English kings among his descendants, and reputedly had the devil among his ancestors.

Let us leave the history of the region at this point and return to the present. Périgord is an agricultural region. Over 40 per cent of the area is forested, fortunately with a mixture of coniferous and deciduous trees, and timber and timber products are one of Périgord's major industries. The local woods also provide the region with fuel, for there is no coal in the Dordogne.

On the plateaux, or 'Causses', sheep are kept in large flocks for their wool, milk, and cheese, and, to a lesser degree, for mutton. The area around Bordeaux and along the Dordogne to St. Emilion and beyond, is wine country, where broad reaches along the river are given over to the cultivation of the grape. For the rest, cattle, nuts, notably walnuts, are exported by the ton, and soft fruits, mostly peaches, plums, apricots, and strawberries. Chestnut trees abound, and their fruit too is a staple food, largely for the feeding of livestock, while the oak, which grows here in a feeble fashion, unlike the spreading giant once so familiar in English acres, nevertheless conceals among its roots that gem of French cuisine, the truffle.

The truffle, which in nature resembles nothing so much as a lump of coke, is, in fact, the result of a fungus disease which afflicts the roots of young oaks. The Périgord farmer therefore plants young oaks in close copses, thus restricting their growth through lack of space, in the hope that among their roots the truffle will flourish.

To locate and extract this black gold, the locals employ trained dogs, the truffle hound, or, less frequently, a pig. Oaks over a certain size cease to produce truffles, and once they grow beyond this point, are ruthlessly chopped down.

The truffle, shaved into thin flakes, makes a feast of any dish, and is the essential ingredient in that speciality of Périgord, the pâté. Indeed, when a dish is described 'à la Périgordienne', this means, garnished with truffles. But we are drifting away from the subject of local industry and off into the more interesting area of food. Back to work! We can return to the pleasures of the table later, when we are on the ground, or in the restaurants.

The Dordogne, in her upper reaches, has been dammed, partly to prevent the water running off the land and being wasted, but mainly for hydro-electricity. These dams are not unattractive, indeed the dam is probably modern man's most satisfying creation. There is some beauty, always, in broad sheets of water. The dams have, however, transformed the river into a series of lakes, and above Argentat, the character of the stream has been totally changed.

Périgord is also a leading producer of tobacco, the rough leaf that, once cured, contributes to that pungent, unmistakable odour one can only find in France. And last but not least, we have wine. Bordeaux has had links with England through the wine trade since the tenth century and before. The reds of the region are justly famous, and the English palate cherishes particularly the fine white wines from the grapes grown in the area between the Dordogne and the Garonne, in the region they call Entre-deux-mers, 'between two rivers'. Within the Dordogne itself, St. Emilion produces the queen of clarets. While, for reasons of economy and profit, much of the fine wine is exported, the locals take good care to keep a share for themselves and their visitors. One can drink, very cheaply, a local *vin ordinaire*, that seems an ambrosia and would cost an excessive amount anywhere else. Nevertheless, just for a treat, the visitor should buy some of the great wines as well. Near Bergerac. on the river, lies Monbazillac, which produces the favourite wine for the local people.

Monbazillac is a sweet, white wine, as are most of the white wines in the district, and I, for one, prefer dry wines; the dry Sauvignon blanc is a favourite. Anyway, the choice, red or white, sweet or dry, is limitless, in this region of excellent wines.

At this point it would be as well to take time to study the end-paper maps. This will give the reader an idea of the Dordogne, of the tilt of the land, and the major cities and towns which surround it.

Within the boundaries of the Department, there are no major cities, and Périgueux is by far the largest town, with a population of over 40,000. Bordeaux is the largest city hereabouts, a major port, the centre of the wine trade, and, since the end of the Second World War, a thriving centre for light and heavy industry of all sorts.

To the north lies Limoges, capital of the Limousin, a fine city,

The Dordogne in the Causse de Martel

once brutally sacked by the Black Prince, and famous for the manufacture of beautiful and delicate porcelain.

To the south beyond Cahors and the cathedral city of Albi, lies Toulouse, which, like Bordeaux, has changed from being a quiet provincial city into a progressive, healthy, industrial town. The French have a deft touch for architecture. They have the knack of blending old and new buildings into a pleasing whole, and a flair for design and style that the Anglo-Saxon, viewing the ruin of many beautiful English cities, can only envy.

Certainly Toulouse, Bordeaux and Limoges and many smaller centres are, even today, pleasant places to visit, sensibly planned and still retaining that timeless air that only comes from cities of considerable antiquity. The smaller towns and valleys of the Dordogne are very pleasing to the eye, and blend in beautifully with the natural splendour of the country.

Périgord leans to the west, and is formed from a limestone plateau, pushed up and tilted sideways by the upheaval of the Massif Central many millions of years ago.

The rivers which seam the country have over the years cut deep wooded valleys in the limestone, down which they tumble, slowing and widening as they run further west. It is the action of these rivers, some running on the surface, others flowing deep underground, that has tunnelled out the deep caves and grottoes of the Dordogne region, home of those primitive hunters who painted the walls of Lascaux and Les Eyzies, and the basis for that recent branch of archaeology, the study of prehistoric man. These caves also gave refuge, in the Middle Ages, to the local people terrorised and dispossessed by the raiding armies of England and France, and the mercenary free companies of men-at-arms, who lived by pillage between campaigns. Some of the caves have been converted into pleasant dwellings that people live in today, but far more have become attractions for the growing number of tourists that visit the Dordogne every summer. Most notable of these attractions is the monolithic abbey of St. Emilion, which has been hacked out of the limey rock. Le Grand Roc at Les Eyzies, on the Vézère, lit by electricity, is always packed, but worth the visit. We shall go there, and visit many more of the underground sights in the Dordogne, and just outside it, at, for instance, Padirac.

It is indeed something of a relief to get out of the car and walk for a while, for the sprawling Dordogne country, seamed by the rivers and ravines between the higher plateaux or 'Causses', can only be explored with any facility by car. The roads are very good, if a little narrow, and very winding as they climb up the valley sides to the higher viewpoints. Everywhere glorious views open up before the traveller, and a temptation never to be resisted is to stop and gaze at the beauty of the scene. In the fine weather that the region enjoys from spring to late autumn, the traveller can see for miles in the clear, unpolluted air. Only when the fierce 'Autun' blows, the stinging hot wind that can scorch the face that is not used to it, does the air become unpleasant. For the rest, it is a land of delights.

Therefore, let us pack suitcase, passport and money, put maps and guides in the glove compartment, and, as they used to put it, 'hie us to the south'.

CHAPTER II

The Road South

There seems to be a tradition that the loading of the car for a trip abroad has to be done in the rain; I, for one, have never started out without wet shoulders and the windscreen wipers going.

Of course, you do not need a car to get to the Dordogne, but one is certainly necessary if you are to see much of the country when you arrive. Besides, France is one of the few countries left where motoring is still a pleasure, where the roads have the speed of a motorway, without the monotony, and, perhaps more important, without the congestion that you find on the winding English roads. The traveller to the Dordogne has a choice of routes, each taking about the same time, but offering a variety of attractions en route. Getting there ought to be part of the fun of a holiday, and in France, to a great degree, this still applies.

The short sea route from Dover to Calais or Boulogne takes a little over the hour, and leads the traveller through St. Omar and Arras, on the Paris road, and so south. This is the road of the Great War, with Vimy Ridge looming up on the left before Arras, and the shattered quiet of the Somme battlefield lying to the right of Baupame, on the road south to Paris, which, needless to say, offers a wide choice of attractions. The road to Paris tends to become very crowded indeed in the summer months. The road from Dieppe heads across some of the most beautiful countryside in Normandy, and has the advantage of offering a wide choice of secondary roads to the traveller who likes to wander, and can take in, for example, Chartres, where the cathedral alone is worth a day of anyone's time, just to see it riding up over the fields, like a great stone ship.

But for me the best route south lies from Cherbourg. It is possible to cross over at night from Southampton, and arrive at the French port in the morning, in time for an early start. That, at least, is the theory. My experience turned out a little different. The boat was due to dock at seven, and, having set my alarm for six, I turned in, anticipating a leisurely shave and breakfast before setting off for a long day's drive.

Emerging from my cabin at six, heading for the bathroom, I found the other doors swinging open, and the cabins empty, while from the car deck below came the sound of cursing, and revving of engines.

A glance through a scuttle showed that the boat had already docked, and a glance down the ladder to the deck below, revealed a wide expanse of empty space in front of my car, and a large crowd of furious motorists trapped behind it.

All thoughts of breakfast fled! Bundling the towel into my hold-all, I leapt into the car, in a snarling silence, and bumped out on to the quay, while furious headlights pursued me through the dawn, down the road to Carantan. The Auberge Normand at Carantan is one of the nicest watering holes in Normandy, where not an eyelid is flickered at disgruntled, unshaven Englishmen marching in at 7 a.m. and demanding hot water and coffee. So soothing were they, that it seemed only natural to book a room for the return trip, and after breakfast, take a stroll round the town. Right next to the Auberge lies a most interesting military museum, dedicated to the 101st U.S. Airborne Division, which captured Carantan from the Germans in 1944. It has an excellent collection of weapons, uniforms, and equipment, and, if you like that sort of thing you will enjoy visiting this museum. Not far from Carantan lies Ste. Mère Eglise, where the 101st's sister division, the 82nd, landed, and they, too, have a museum. Apart from this, Ste. Mère Eglise is worth a visit, if only for the magnificent church that stands in the main square. But we must get on.

The route south takes one past Coutances and Laval in a long sweep down to Angers, on the Loire. Angers is relevant to our story, for it was for generations the ancestral home of the Angevin Counts of Anjou, who ruled in the Dordogne, and one of whom, Fulk, managed to get himself related to the Devil.

It appears that, a long time ago, Count Fulk went away on a journey and returned, after some years, married to a beautiful lady. They seemed very happy and in course of time had four children, two boys and two girls. Only two things about his wife bothered the Count. Firstly, she appeared to have no relatives, and while one cannot imagine that they had baby-sitting problems, in an age when everyone of a certain class knew everyone else, her lack of kin seemed a little odd. Secondly, she seemed very reluctant to attend Mass, which, what with the constant feast days and setting an example to the lower orders, took up a lot of the nobility's time. The Lady always managed to get out of the Mass somehow, until one day the Count, very uneasily, decided to make an issue of it.

When next she entered the church, he made two of his largest knights stand on the hem of her cloak. All went well until the bell tinkled for elevation of the Host, at which point the Lady began to scream in agony. Tearing herself loose from the cloak, she seized two of her children and flew out of the window, and neither she nor the children were ever seen again, and her husband, not surprisingly, went into decline, and soon died.

It transpired that his wife was Melusine, the Devil's daughter, and from her two remaining children by the Count, all the later Counts of Anjou were descended. When Count Geoffrey, father of Henry II of England, reigned in Angers, the story of his descent from the devil was known everywhere, even if few intelligent people believed it. The Angevins were a ferocious family, and, it appears, were not ashamed of their devilish origins. Geoffrey has another claim to fame for, like all medieval kings, he was a great hunter and loved all aspects of the chase, particularly hawking. To improve the cover for birds, he was in the habit of carrying with him cuttings of gorse and broom which he would plant in any likely spot; this habit earned him a curious nickname that remained with his line for nearly 400 years. His followers called him the Broom Planter, or Plantagenet, *genet* being the French word for gorse or broom.

Count Geoffrey was a mild and honourable man, and when he died at the early age of thirty-nine, he left to his son Henry a contented and prosperous county. But blood, in the end, will tell, as we shall see.

Anjou in the twelfth century was, in itself, one of the great feudal counties of France, but Count Geoffrey had also inherited from his mother the adjoining county of Maine, and he married Matilda, daughter of Henry I, King of England. By marrying her, he became, as her husband, King of England and Duke of Normandy.

Samaur on the Loire

29

However, Geoffrey had few territorial ambitions and had no great love for his wife. Besides, the English, on the death of Henry I, elected Stephen to the throne, and a cruel war, between Stephen and Matilda, raged in England for twenty years, during which time, as a chronicler put it, 'God and his Saints slept'. Geoffrey wanted no part of these brawls, and ruled his counties and the Duchy of Normandy, as an inheritance for his son, Henry, who was born in 1133. This was the Henry who was later to marry the beautiful and wilful Eleanor of Aquitaine, and become Henry II of England.

Angers lies on the River Maine, a tributary of the Loire, which the road south crosses just south of Angers and then forks left towards Saumur. Saumur is one of the great garrison towns of France, famous down the ages as a cavalry centre. Happily, it has a more enjoyable feature to recommend it today, for this is the place to stop and enjoy that very delectable, dry white wine that comes from the Loire, Muscadet.

Most wines take their name from the district or vineyard where they are grown, but Muscadet takes its name from the grape itself, a plump, white, juicy, fruit that grows all along the valley, and makes a remarkably fine wine drunk throughout France, but especially in Brittany and Normandy where it complements the excellent seafood for which those provinces are famous.

The Loire flows through Saumur, and once across the river we enter old Languedoc. Nowadays, that once great area, has shrunk in name to a small Department on the Mediterranean coast, but, when the Plantagenets ruled, the whole area south of the Loire reflected an air and an attitude much warmer and more volatile than in the lands to the north.

Henry II died at the castle at Chinon on the Loire, alone and broken-hearted, after the defection of his youngest son, John. His body, dressed in borrowed finery, was brought the twenty miles to Fontevrault, mausoleum of the Angevin dynasty, and the next stop on our way south.

The religious order of Fontevrault was established in 1101 and in the twelfth century, the abbey at Fontevrault contained a monastery, and a nunnery. The superior was an abbess. Henry II once considered sending his son John to be a monk there, for John

Effigy of Richard Coeur de Lion

was always interested in religious matters and might, had things turned out differently, become a very good Archbishop, instead of a remarkably bad king.

The abbey became a favourite foundation of the Angevins, and was frequently in receipt of benefits from them, usually made to atone for their latest crime, but, in all events, the abbey prospered. Henry II was buried there in 1189, and Richard Coeur-de-Lion joined him ten years later, to be followed by his mother, Eleanor, who returned to Fontevrault in her old age and died there in 1204. The abbey has suffered the usual damage, both from age and the depredations of fanatics, but it has been beautifully maintained, and is well worth a visit.

The effigies of Eleanor, Henry, Richard, and Isobel, John's wife, are kept in the abbey church. These effigies are particularly interesting because they still carry their original paint, and are quite handsomely coloured. Nowadays we are used to simple white-washed churches relieved perhaps with oak, brass, and some stained glass. The medieval churches were not like that at all. They glowed with colour, rich frescoes on the walls, bright brasses and the tombs of the local nobility and gentry, the altar cloths glowing below the cross. Much goodwill was stored up for the next world by decorating God's home in this one. The colourful effigies of the Angevins are just a brief reminder of the splendour that has gone. It is strange to think of them now, for those effigies at Fontevrault are all that remain of a family that once ruled most of Western Europe, and whose quarrels shook empires.

The Angevin family, and their descendants the Plantagenets, ruled England and, intermittently, much of France, from 1133 until 1453. In the end, torn apart by their own quarrels and hunted down relentlessly by the usurping Tudors, their line has been totally extinguished and all that energy and power has drained away.

In the seventeenth century a judge summed it up when giving the verdict on the also defunct Earldom of Oxford. *'Where is Bohun? Where is Mowbray? Nay last and most of all, where is Plantagenet? There must be an end to names and territories and whatsoever is terrain, for they are entombed in the urns and sepulchres of brief mortality.'* What an epitaph!

From Fontevrault the road leads down to Poitiers, once the greatest city in the Duchy of Aquitaine.

Modern Poitiers is a healthy industrial city, with large factories and office buildings standing around the town. It was near here, in 1356, that Edward of Woodstock, later known as the Black Prince, fought a French army that barred his route to Bordeaux, and crushed it utterly, taking prisoner the French King, John the Good, and most of the knights and barons who survived.

The Prince had been on a *chevauchée*, a great plundering raid across France, when the French army overtook him near Poitiers. Ladened with booty that they were reluctant to abandon, the English army took up a defensive position, in their usual harrow formation, with men-at-arms in the middle and the fearsome English archers on the flanks.

Remembering the chaos the English bowmen had caused the mounted French chivalry at Crécy eleven years before, John dismounted his main divisions, or 'battles', and led them on foot,

Inside the abbey at Fontrevault

against the English line. This was a disastrous mistake, for it is one thing to stand and fight in full armour and quite another to march half a mile in it, under the arrow storm. Moreover, the Prince had kept a force of mounted knights under the Gascon, Captal de Buch, who charged the French from the flank, and routed them, the French King finding himself a prisoner of the English.

It is a curious nickname, the Black Prince. No one called him that in his lifetime, and indeed the first noticeable reference to it, and that in passing, is in Shakespeare's *Henry V*, where the French King hearing of Henry's landings, says

> 'Think we King Harry strong,
> The kindred of him have been fleshed
> upon us;
> For he is bred out of that bloody
> strain, that haunted us in our familiar
> paths
> When Cressy battle fatally was struck
> And all our princes captive by the hand of
> that black name,
> Edward, black prince of Wales.'

Some have it that the Prince wore black armour, which is unlikely, and others that the name arose from the gloom and despondency he spread among his enemies, which is perhaps more credible. The most probable explanation, however, is that black was his favourite colour. The Prince of Wales crest, which was adopted from that of Bohemia after Crécy, has three white feathers on a black field, and it is recorded that when the Prince brought the captured King John into London, he rode beside him on a black pony, while the King rode, as was proper, a white warhorse. Or perhaps to satisfy the purist we should say a grey warhorse. Why is it that devotees of the horse persist in calling an animal grey that is patently white, and a hunting coat pink, that is obviously red? It may be a way of sorting out the right people from the *hoi-polloi*, but why the rest of us indulge these whims I cannot imagine.

At Poitiers the traveller has two choices, either to go south via Lussac and Limoges, or take the western route through Angoulême. The latter is probably faster, for it is being developed into a dual

The Arms of John Chandos

35

carriageway along most of the route to take the products of Poitiers down to the great port of Bordeaux. It also leads the traveller through the Cognac country, which no lover of brandy would readily miss.

On this journey, however, we will go via Lussac for it contains sights not unconnected with the parts we shall come to further south, and brings us into the Dordogne by a more historic series of landmarks.

By the bridge at Lussac on the Poitiers–Limoges road lies an inn with a sign that brought me to a halt. *Argent, à pile gules.* A strange device like a red wedge, on a white background, that no one would know today, but in the fourteenth century there was not a knight in Christendom that would not have recognised the red pile of Chandos. One-eyed John Chandos, Constable of Aquitaine, friend and tutor of the Black Prince, was the most famous knight of his day, and his exploits were a source of song and story during his lifetime and for years after his death. He fought in all the wars of Edward III, and the Black Prince, at Poitiers, and at Najera when the Prince took an army into Spain to help Pedro the Cruel over-throw his bastard half brother, Henry of Trastamare, and got nothing out of it but the great ruby that glows today in the English Imperial State Crown, and the recurrent dysentery that was to wreck his health and temper, and finally kill him.

During the Prince's long illness, John Chandos led the armies of Aquitaine against the ever bolder invasions of the French, who had themselves found an inspiring leader in Bertrand de Guesclin. It was a war of ambush and flight, with no great battles, but many minor skirmishes, and in one of these, by the bridge at Lussac, John Chandos was killed, stabbed through the visor on his blind side. Even his enemies, the French, mourned his passing, and helped bury him on a little mound near the place where he was killed.

Later on, a monument was erected and still stands there today, that and an inn sign being the only remembrances remaining to one who, in his time, was the most noble knight in all the world.

CHAPTER III

Into the Dordogne

At Bellac, twenty-five miles north of Limoges, we stand on the doorstep of the Dordogne, and inside the Limousin plateau.

This is, like the Dordogne itself, farming country, with little industry other than that connected with the land. Most of the farming is pastoral, mainly cattle-rearing for beef, and the fields that border the roads are full of cattle, usually the light brown type of France, with only the occasional herd of Hereford milkers, to add variety. Sheep are here in abundance, rather smaller than those of the English South Down flocks, and reared mainly for their wool.

The fields are bordered by deep woods while, as we move south and the rise and fall of the land becomes more pronounced, whole hillsides are given over to forestry. Happily, most of the trees are deciduous, oak, ash, birch, and beech, and their variety makes the woods a beautiful sight, avoiding the monotony of evergreen coniferous plantations. Timber is another of the local, rural industries, and logging operations are apparent everywhere, the roads spattered with heavy mud from the wheels of the tractors.

Bellac itself is a small pleasant town overlooking the valley of the Vincou, the town rising up in a series of layers from the floor of the valley, and topped by a magnificent Romanesque church. From the south, the views of Bellac across the green valley are very beautiful, while inside the town quiet, narrow streets wind up and down, and give deep and welcome shade on a hot day.

Bellac is the birthplace of the playwright Jean Giraudoux, who was born in the town in 1882. A curious sight is the Hôtel de Ville, once the town's castle, and still retaining many thirteenth and sixteenth century features, including watchtowers on the walls. Small gardens and a weekly market add to the charm of the town, which is a good centre for touring the Limousin.

Bellac lies on one of the main roads south and on summer week-ends endures some formidable traffic congestion. It is one of the pleasures of France that, if you leave the main roads, the smaller ones are just as fast and frequently deserted. From Bellac, we can take the side roads to our next destination, Oradour sur Glane.

The road runs along the tops of the ridges, and we are rising steadily now, raised up far above the land with fine views on either side. The only blots on the landscape are power cables, on their attendant pylons. The upper reaches of the Dordogne river have been dammed in several places as a source of hydro-electric power and the cables take the power away to the factories of the north, for the Dordogne provides France with a significant amount of the energy she needs. Be that as it may, pylons are no attraction, wherever they appear, and here, as they stretch their way across the country, they definitely detract from the view. Fortunately they are not as numerous as they might be, and the glorious countryside more than compensates for their presence. The little village of Blonde, which lies on the cross-country road ten miles from Oradour, has a fine example of a fortified church. These churches are by no means uncommon in this part of France, but the one at Blonde is a particularly fine example. The church dates from the twelfth century, and was fortified in the sixteenth, probably during the Wars of Religion. The presence of these fortified churches gives some indication of the warfare that raged across this land for centuries, and reached a terrible climax in the last War, at Oradour.

The Limousin plain, from Blonde, seems much flatter than it actually is, for the wooded hills conceal the valleys, and level out the undulations of the landscape, which is already taking on some aspects of the warmer south. Even palms can occasionally be seen growing stumpily in some sheltered spot. Wild flowers also flourish, with tall purple foxgloves edging the roads, and daisies speckling the fields among the drowsing cattle.

The French have been very clever and successful in reconstruct-ing their towns and valleys after the ravages of war. This is particularly so in Normandy, where over 5,000 towns and villages were totally destroyed in the Second World War and yet have been so well rebuilt, that they look as if they have stood for centuries. This is not the case with the new village of Oradour sur Glane. The

Oradour sur Glane

houses look painfully new, and the whole village overlooks the ruin of the old.

George Santayana said that a nation that forgets its history is doomed to relive it. That alone is good enough reason for visiting Oradour, which was the scene of one of the most bloody massacres in history, not in the Dark Ages, but within our own lifetime.

On the afternoon of 10th June 1944, troops of the German 2nd S.S. Division (Das Reich) surrounded Oradour. The division had been refitting in the South of France when the Allies landed on D-Day, and was hurrying north to join the fighting round the Normandy beaches. All the way north they had been harassed, ambushed, and sniped by the Maquis and near Oradour two of their outriders had been killed. The division commander decided to carry out a reprisal.

The 2nd S.S. rounded up the entire population of the village and paraded them in the main square. Then they separated the men from the women and children and the killing began. The men were machine-gunned, and only three managed to escape. The women and the children were locked in the church, which was set alight, and the whole village was put to the torch.

This was no reprisal, this was wholesale murder. The Germans killed 642 people, over 200 of them school-children. They shot the village priest, and both the doctors, and old Marthe who was over seventy years old and little Mayre who was only six. They shot her sisters, too.

Then the S.S. left, and Oradour's terrible story leaked out to the world. A low wall now surrounds the village, and all has been left as the local people found it when rescuers began to reach the village after the S.S. had departed. The main street runs between the roofless houses, many with charred shutters still swinging in the windows. Inside, one can see the twisted remains of family possessions, a sewing machine, the treadle buckled by the heat of the fire, a bicycle rusting on a wall, a car still parked in a garage. The railway lines still run down the street, and the wind sighs quietly in the telephone wires. Inside the church, the altar still stands, with bullet marks pocking the stones. Oradour is a sad and somehow beautiful place, where even the visitors seemed subdued. Or most of them.

I was back at my car, wondering how civilised men could bring themselves to do such things, when a large coach entered the car park, from which emerged a large party of middle-aged Germans. In view of Santayana's remark this seemed reasonable, but I was still there writing my notes when they reappeared. Outside the entrance of the village which bears the words, *Souviens-toi*, 'Remember', they formed a group, and with much good-natured jostling and laughter proceeded to take each other's photographs. What the French thought of this performance I cannot imagine, but I drove away thinking that, to put it mildly, the Germans are a curious people.

From Oradour the road south follows the valley of the Vienne, a wide and pleasant river, and we go with it as far as the village of Aixe, on the road between Limoges and Périgueux, where we turn south for Châlus. It is also possible to proceed through Limoges, the capital of the Limousin, veer off at this point, and head to the east to Bourganeuf, which is a pleasant town with a curious story.

Bourganeuf was, for a number of years at the end of the fifteenth century, the home and prison of the Turkish Prince, Djem. Djem, or, as the French prefer to call him, Zim Zim, was the brother of the Turkish Sultan, Bayezid II. Djem had rebelled unsuccessfully against his brother, and on the collapse of his revolt had fled, for fear of the bowstring that awaited him in Constantinople, and taken shelter with the Knights of St. John of Jerusalem, the Military Order then based in Rhodes.

The Order was organised into companies called *Langues*, and it was the Langue of Auvergne which took the Prince into custody and transferred him to their castle of Bourganeuf, where he lived, in considerable splendour, while his brother, the Sultan, happily paid the Knights 40,000 ducats a year to keep him prisoner. In 1489 Djem and his ransom were transferred to the custody of the then Pope, Innocent VIII. He became a familiar figure in Rome and lived in great comfort in the Vatican.

Fate, however, had not finished with Djem. In 1494 the French King Charles VIII invaded Italy. Charles was more than a little mad, and his intention was to annex the Kingdom of Naples and use it as a base for a crusade against the Turk. On his way through Rome, Charles demanded the surrender of Djem from the Borgia

Pope Alexander VI, intending to use the Prince during his crusade, and Alexander had no option but to hand him over.

The Sultan had offered a considerable sum to ensure that his brother took no part in the French King's crusade, and before handing the Prince over, Alexander administered a poison to him. Or so the legend has it. In fact Djem did not die until a month after he left Rome, and then probably of the plague. One wonders what thoughts Djem must have had during these long years in captivity, passed as he was, like a parcel, from one hand to another, to die at last, alone, among the Infidel.

Châlus is another of these little hilltop towns dominated by a castle. The castle at Châlus is of particular interest to the English because it was here that Eleanor of Aquitaine's third and favourite son, Richard Coeur-de-Lion, King of England, was mortally wounded, on 6th April 1199.

The Lord of Châlus had found a hoard of treasure buried on his land, but refused to share it with his liege lord, Richard, who took a party of *routiers*, under their captain, Mercadier, to demand it. While reconnoitring the walls, the King was struck in the shoulder by a crossbow bolt and died a few days later of blood poisoning. He was forty-three.

Mercadier took the castle before the King died, and the man who had fired the fatal arrow was brought before the King, to plead for mercy. Richard forgave him and ordered Mercadier to set him free, but, after Richard died, the *routier* took the archer to Eleanor. She had no mercy for the man who had killed her son, and had the archer skinned alive.

There is very little left of the Castle of Châlus, except for some of the bailey walls, and an enormous tower, from which wonderful views can be obtained over the little town and the surrounding countryside.

Leaving Châlus we go south again, via Ladignac to see the great castle of Jumilhac-le-Grand. These *ac* endings are very common hereabouts in the Dordogne, and date back to Roman times, being derived from the word *acqua*, water. Water is such a feature of the Dordogne that it is not surprising to find it attached to place names. Passing through the country the traveller will quickly notice the many small artificial lakes or ponds which are sprinkled across the landscape. The region has an adequate rainfall, but the rain runs quickly off the land, and there would be problems in high summer without these little lakes to store the water. They also seem to contribute to the French countryman's great love, *la pêche*, for most have a boat on them, or are fringed with fishermen at week-ends.

A view of Châlus

Another feature, apart from ponds, are walnut trees. Nuts of all sorts, but particularly walnuts, are a speciality of the region, and the best Périgord dishes are either flavoured with truffle or cooked in walnut oil. Singly, or in little groups, the walnut tree is a common sight, and few fields seem to be without one.

The castle of Jumilhac-le-Grand stands on a hill above the river

Isle, a river that runs down through Périgueux, and eventually into the Dordogne at Libourne. At Jumilhac, it is no more than 50 yards wide and slow moving, winding slowly round the cliff on which the castle stands.

The castle itself is spectacular, a huge building crowned with the usual Périgordien cupolas. The castle was begun in the thirteenth

A view of Jumilhac

century but added to continually for the next three centuries, until it reached the massive proportions it retains today.

From Jumilhac, we head south-east to the village of Angoisse, where, for those who like good food in a quiet and charming setting, Chez Marcel, in the central square, is not to be missed. The quiet in these Dordogne farming villages is one of their great attractions, especially around midday when many of the villages

44

seem quite deserted while the inhabitants, presumably, give themselves over to the pleasures of the table.

From Angoisse we go east, out of the Dordogne for a while and into the neighbouring department of Corrèze to the castle of Pompadour. The beautiful and desirable Marquise de Pompadour, mistress of Louis XV, never actually visited Pompadour, let alone lived there. She would have found it much too dull and provincial. In spite of this, the town has done very well in the last 200 years from her name and reputation, but since she did pretty well for herself as Madame de Pompadour, this seems only fair.

Jeanne, Marquise de Pompadour, was born plain Antoinette Poisson, in 1721, and first met her royal lover in 1745. She was the daughter of a municipal clerk. Her father was caught in some unlawful speculation and was forced to flee abroad, and during his absence her mother became the mistress of Normant de Tournhem, who educated her children, and married Jeanne to his nephew. Jeanne was instructed in all the social graces and found her way into the then fashionable *salons* of Madame Deffand and Madame Geoffrin. She attended a masque at Versailles, at which, by some chance, both she and the King wore the same costume, being disguised, of all things, as yew-trees. They therefore had plenty to talk about, and very little to do, and within a few months Jeanne became Louis' chief mistress and Marquise de Pompadour. She was elegant, witty, and very popular, even with Louis' wife.

'If we must have mistresses,' said the Queen, 'I am glad it is Madame de Pompadour.'

The Pompadour is better remembered for her patronage of the arts, and under her influence Paris became the artistic capital of Europe. The porcelain factory at Sèvres was started at her instigation, and she was instrumental in directing work to the tapestry works of Gobelin and Aubusson. She also protected the writer Diderot, and the members of his circle, then engaged in the mammoth Encyclopedia. The Pompadour was an intelligent woman who saw quite clearly what would happen unless the Ancien Régime changed its ways, and gave more freedom to the people.

Après moi le déluge is her best remembered aphorism. She was the King's mistress for five years, and his firm friend for twenty, and yet it is recorded that, when she died in 1764 and her body

The Chateau de Pompadour

was removed from Versailles, Louis watched from a balcony without a sign of regret.

Near Pompadour, and well worth a visit, is the little village of Segur-le-Château, home of the Comtes de Segur who were leading soldiers and courtiers at Versailles during the reigns of Louis XV and XVI, and later, Napoleon. One Comte de Segur who became Marshal of France and Minister of War to Louis XVI, placed such value in blue blood as a source of military ability that he decreed that no man could be an officer in the French army unless his coat of arms displayed four quarterings of the nobility. What Napoleon would have made of that is anyone's guess, for his only requirement, apart from ability, was that a general should be lucky.

Pompadour, which we now leave behind us, to return to Dordogne, is a pleasant place, a centre for horse breeding, with a small race-course opposite the Château, and ample signs of successful exploitation of the tourist. We go now through the delightfully named village of St. Bonnet, and turn west towards Hautefort. This takes us across the valleys of various small rivers, and reminds us yet again that we are on a plateau, or rather a series of plateaux, none particularly flat on top, all well wooded, but there because the rivers have carved the valleys below the level of the land, and not because the land is, of itself, particularly mountainous. Coming from St. Bonnet we approach the little town of Badefols-d'Ans.

Badefols has a wonderful martial castle with machicolated walls and a roofed keep. Standing, as usual, on a hilltop it dominates the surrounding countryside, and glares across the valley at the towers of Hautefort.

Hautefort was devastated by fire in 1968 and is only now being repaired, but for size, setting, and splendour, not less than for a long and curious history, Hautefort is unique in Périgord. One is prepared for the size since the castle dominates the surrounding countryside from whichever direction you approach, but one cannot be prepared for the beauty.

The setting itself, above the little town, is superb, and closer to the walls the castle rises up, with lawns beneath the battlements and with beautiful well-kept gardens along the terraces of the castle, below the towers.

Hautefort has a park, a drawbridge, a dry moat, a knot garden, and a wonderful arboured walk before the gate. A huge forecourt of carefully raked gravel sets off grey-yellow walls that sparkle in the sunlight. Hautefort is delightful. On the site of the present château stood, in the twelfth century, the castle of Bertrand de Born, 'the friend and enemy of Kings'.

Bertrand was a powerful baron, a troubadour and a trouble-maker. He had charm, talent, and not a single moral scruple, being, in short, the sort of person nowadays very much admired. His

Hautefort

particular genius lay in keeping the Angevins at each other's throats, though this could not have been a very difficult task, and he did this by composing *sirvantes*, or political songs. He was in modern terms, a satirist.

Bertrand's problem lay in the fact that his father had left the lands and castle at Hautefort jointly to his two sons, Bertrand and

Constantine. Since each wished to oust the other, Constantine swore loyalty to the Old King, Henry II, while Bertrand approached anyone who would support him, usually one of Henry's sons.

He managed to rouse the Young King Henry against his father, and indeed with his silver tongue he kept everything in a satisfactory state of turmoil for years. The only one he failed to influence was Richard Coeur-de-Lion, whom he nicknamed in a *sirvante* Richard Yea and Nay. But with the rest of the Angevin family he managed well enough.

As any modern satirist knows, a state of turmoil is necessary for his success. If the state is at peace and contented, his influence is gone. Bertrand's influence on the Young King Henry kept the latter either at war with his brother Richard, or in rebellion against his father, the Old King. Richard, who was no man's fool, knew where the root cause of the trouble lay, and when the Young Henry, still in rebellion against his father, died in 1183, Richard took his knights to Hautefort and drove Bertrand out, putting the more amenable Constantine in his place. It was no good though. Bertrand went and begged forgiveness of the Old King Henry, who, still grief-stricken over the death of his heir, gave him back his castle. Later in life, one would like to think, overcome with remorse, Bertrand left Hautefort and entered a monastery, where he eventually died. In the later Middle Ages Bertrand gained increasing notoriety, comparable almost with that accredited to Machiavelli. Dante, in particular, thought Bertrand to be a fiend and features him, in Hell, in one of the Divine Comedies. Colourful Hautefort, now being carefully restored is, with the history of Bertrand, a wonderful place to visit.

From Hautefort, our way lies to the south-east, across the hills again to the far corner of the Dordogne, and the town of Brive-La-Gaillarde.

Brive lies at the meeting place of the roads from Limoges to Toulouse, and Bordeaux to Clermont-Ferrand. It is therefore a traffic nightmare, and best visited on a Sunday, when at least the commercial traffic is not so heavy. Long experience has taught that cities should, where possible, be visited on Sundays, but popular tourist centres and sites should be visited during the week, when at least some of the people are working. By sticking to this practice wherever possible, I have managed to see most of the things I want to see in peace and quiet, and with comparative ease. I do not care for large towns, and they get scant attention in this book. They are, usually, so obvious that even the casual visitor cannot miss them.

As large towns go, and Brive is not *that* large, with a population of about 50,000, it is a pleasant place, and an excellent centre for visiting places, notably the prehistoric sites in Corrèze. Most of these, however, lie further east away from the Dordogne, and we must now turn west again, along the road to Périgueux.

CHAPTER IV

To Périgueux and the Périgord Blanc

The road from Brive to Périgueux runs for much of its length along
the valley of the river Vézère, which flows south from St. Bonnet
and then turns west for a while through Terrasson-la-Villedieu,
before it turns south again towards Les Eyzies.

Terrasson is a quaint place with two bridges crossing the river,
and marks the boundary between the Limousin and the old province

The medieval footbridge at Terrasson

of Quercy. The road to Périgueux crosses to the north bank of the Vézère by the modern road bridge, which gives a good view of the narrow, gracious footbridge, wide enough only for pack-animals, and built in the twelfth century.

From here we pass through Rastignac which has, or had, a magnificent château, which was supposed to have inspired the architecture of the White House in Washington. In 1944, the château was set alight by the Germans, as a reprisal for Maquis activity in the area, and is only now being restored.

At St. Laurent, on the right-hand road to Périgueux, lies what can only be described as a pâté farm. Here, in long cages, are kept the geese whose livers provide the basis for the great speciality of the region, pâté de foie-gras. At the risk of putting you off the dish for life, the process should be lightly described. Briefly, the geese are force-fed until their livers become enlarged and degenerate, at which time they are killed. The liver with the addition of slivers of truffle, becomes a highly prized delicacy, and commands a considerable price. At St. Laurent, in a shop between the cages, tins and bottles of foie-gras and other regional specialities are bought eagerly by passing travellers, seeming quite unperturbed by the scores of beady eyes watching them from behind the wire netting. The French, curiously enough, are not such great foie-gras eaters as the English, probably because of the price. Foie-gras tends to be a seasonal dish in France eaten particularly at Christmas, hence, perhaps, the old rhyme which tells that

'Christmas is coming, the goose is getting fat,
Please put a penny in the blind man's hat'.

A turn off the road here takes us to Athur, a small village which contains a Lanterne des Morts. These curious, hollow, pillarbox type structures are very rare, and no one seems to know when or why they were first erected. Certainly the one at Athur is at least 300 years old, and probably much older. However, in spite of doubts about the origin, the locals are still putting the Lanterne to use. A watch-fire is lit at night whenever anyone of prominence dies, and from here, the highest spot in Athur, the Lanterne can be seen for miles around. It was last lit, in mourning, on the death of General de Gaulle.

Lanterne des Morts at Athur

53

Périgueux and the Cathedral of St. Front

From Athur, the back roads take us down, across the Isle to Périgueux, and the view from the bridge over the river gives the traveller a startling sight of the great cathedral of St. Front. St. Front himself was an apostle sent by St. Peter to evangelise Périgord. His tomb at Périgueux is mentioned as early as the seventh century, and was destroyed by the Huguenots in 1575.

St. Front is one of those places which, although one has never seen it before, looks terribly familiar. Then you realise that it is like all the posters one has ever seen of the Blue Mosque in Constantinople. It even has a stunted form of minaret, jutting out around the domed cupolas of the roof. As so often happens, distance lends enchantment and close to, St. Front is a bore. Inside, it is a vast, cold, stone cavern dimly lit by the flickering candles of the faithful, and a place to get out of as quickly as possible.

Périgueux itself though is delightful. The old city which clusters

54

close to the cathedral is a maze of narrow medieval streets and alleyways, which reek of olden times. Unlike some medieval cities, such as Carcassonne, Périgueux is big enough and prosperous enough not to rely on tourism for a livelihood, with the result that many of its buildings are still lived in by families, or used as offices or workshops by small firms. This area would make a delightful artists' quarter, it has all the feel of one, and, happily, those buildings that have felt their age and were crumbling are being carefully restored.

Périgueux is the capital city of the Dordogne, as it was once the capital of Périgord. It has a population of some 50,000 and is the ideal centre for a holiday, or for exploring the Dordogne, situated as it is practically in the middle of the Department.

The city is a gastronomic centre, an exporter of high quality foodstuffs, like pâté, and the home of several restaurants that specialise in the local cuisine. Notable among these are the Restaurant Léon, and the La Bousse, which, while hardly cheap, are well worth the money.

Périgueux suffered considerably in the Middle Ages, and during the Wars of Religion, when Catholic and Huguenot each captured the place in their turn and did considerable damage in the process.

Away from the old quarter, around St. Front, in what is now the more modern part of the town, on the road to Angoulême, are some even older sights, including the fine church of St. Etienne de la Cité which until 1669 used to be the old cathedral, although it was badly damaged by the Huguenots in 1577. Near St. Etienne lies all that is left of the old Roman amphitheatre that could once seat over 20,000 people and is now a public garden. The amphitheatre's destruction began as early as the third century AD and now only the domed gateways to the old arena are left, through which one passes out to the street. It seems strange to walk along a passageway that once gave entrance to an anxious Christian, or a hungry lion.

Just outside, I got lost, and appealed to a man sitting on a bench for information. He knocked my map aside and asked abruptly,

'Etes-vous Allemand?'

'Mais non, pas du tout! Je suis Anglais.'

'Ah,' he smiled, 'an English, we must have a drink.'

We had several, and lunch.

Paul was an old Maquisard, a member of the wartime Resistance. His dislike of the Germans was only just ahead of his dislike of the French.

'After the war, in the Auvergne, we had parades. There were more Maquisards in 1946 than there ever were in the war! And the salute, at the parades, was by people who helped the Germans. So I left, and came here to Périgueux. There may be collaborators here, but I don't know them.'

All the Dordogne, indeed most of central France, was Maquis country and towards the end of the occupation most hilltops had a little band of resistors. Memorials to Maquisards shot by 'the Germans', noticeably never by 'the Nazis', are everywhere.

The subject of the war and the Resistance comes up frequently in conversation with local people. The war was one of the few things that the French and English have shared, but, apart from that, there seems to be a need to explain, to tell you how it was. Britain, fortunately, was never occupied, and the wise man stays quiet and just listens, for the attitude of the French is contradictory.

After due acknowledgement that there were brave men in the Resistance, there lies an undercurrent of annoyance. The activities of the Maquis certainly stirred the Germans up, but then their methods of repression tended to be Draconian. Many ordinary people, who just wished to endure the Occupation as best they could, suffered from the curfews, the searches, the deportations, the taking and shooting of hostages, and disapproved of the activities of these men who, if patriotic, were often little more than bandits. The Maquis killed two men of the 2nd S.S. Division, and what happened at Oradour as a result has already been mentioned. Was it worth it? Did all the Resistance activity shorten the war by even one day?

Paul is aware of this attitude, and even accepts it. His bitterness, and it runs deep, is for quite a different reason. To him, and I think rightly, the Resistance was necessary for France, for her morale, and, an unfamiliar word today, for her honour. France could not remain subservient for five years, and then be saved by others. Moreover, the Resistance helped to compensate for those who informed and collaborated in the police or in the Melice, the paramilitary secret police that served the Gestapo. There were wild men in the Maquis, and maybe some did raid tobacconists, and hold up

The abbey at Chancelade

57

banks, but they also fought for France, and died for her if they had to.

Chancelade, just off the road to Brantôme outside Périgueux, is an interesting place. The abbey church there is still functioning, and evening service was in progress when I arrived. The twelfth century abbey is interesting to the present-day visitor, because it has retained many of the original monastic features. It lives, and only the monks are missing. It has cloisters, a refectory, a guest wing, for monasteries were the hotels of medieval Europe, and most interesting of all, a well-watered carp-pond. What with Fridays and Sundays and innumerable feast days, which were really fast days, the medieval monastery had a great appetite for fish. All abbeys had fish-ponds, and the huge slow carp was the popular dish. Baked carp was, from the right cook, a dish fit for a king, and very gratifying for an abbot. The top of the tower at Chancelade can be seen from the Périgueux to Brantôme road, and the diversion is well worth while.

Further along we come to the village of Château-L'Evêque. The château is now a large and modern hotel. Seen from the road it is a most imposing sight, and while the hotel is very comfortable, the atmosphere of a medieval fortress still remains.

The attractions of the Dordogne are so many and varied that, in themselves, they justify the trip. They have, however, one great advantage in that they provide the traveller with a reason for travelling across the region, where every turn brings a fresh new scene, and every view a new delight. One is well advised to forsake the main roads wherever possible and strike out across country, in the general direction of your destination. On the side roads you can travel for miles without seeing another car, let alone another human being, and the blessing of solitude is not one to be missed, if it lies close at hand.

Any direction vaguely north-east, off the Périgueux to Brantôme road above Château-L'Evêque, will eventually bring one to Bourdeilles, and Bourdeilles is a gem.

The setting, the castle, the tranquillity, all combine to make Bourdeilles an absolute must for any traveller. The setting in the valley of the swift, shallow, sparkling Dronne is superb, and the little town nestles, all white walls and red roofs, at the foot of a towering limestone, yellow castle, round the walls of which the river curves and bubbles. A mill beneath the castle walls parts the stream which in passing turns the mill wheel, and sends the water rushing under the old curved bridge. Anyone would wax lyrical about Bourdeilles, and still fail to describe it fully.

The castle at Bourdeilles, which dates from the thirteenth century, was built by the French and surrendered to the English by St. Louis when he returned to them the French lands lost by King John. Bertrand de Guesclin, France's Fabian general, recaptured it in the following century and it remained in French hands thereafter. The medieval *donjon* or tower is open to the public and a considerable climb is rewarded with views over the Dronne valley. From the river one gets a view of the fine Renaissance building added to the castle in the sixteenth century and the relic of a sad little tale.

Catherine de Medici decided to take her son Charles on a tour of his kingdom, and the news caused a great stir throughout the land with every landowner hoping for a royal visit. The Lady of Bourdeilles hired architects and masons and had the fine building we see today erected to house the court, but they never came! The Queen saw no reason to visit good Catholics already loyal and passed by to woo less staunch allies. Clearly the loyal got little attention in that or any other age, while those of doubtful faith get flattered.

The writer Pierre de Bourdeilles was born in the castle in 1540. In his early life he was a soldier, and fought at Jarnac in 1569. He was a leading figure at the French court and a confidant of Henry II's wife, Mary, later Queen of Scots. After Jarnac, however, he returned to the abbey at Brantôme, and, taking the town as his pen-name, began to write. His writings were anything but contemplative, and his *Les Dames Galantes*, which gives a detailed, not to say intimate, portrait of various goings on at the court of the Valois, delighted his contemporaries and has been read with much scurrilous amusement ever since. Bourdeilles, or Brantôme, died in 1614.

Brantôme is not far from Bourdeilles and is reached by a road flanked by the Dronne on one side and by limestone cliffs on the other. Down the centuries the river, hollowing out the valley, has carved deep holes in the limestone, undercutting the cliffs horizontally in places, until it is a wonder that they do not collapse. Near Brantôme, the caves in the cliffs have either been turned into homes, or incorporated into larger outside dwellings. Cliff homes

Brantôme

are not peculiar to the Dordogne and indeed one can see them along the Loire, but they are very common here, and a feature worth looking out for.

Brantôme is a picturesque place with elegant buildings overlooking the Dronne and a fine abbey, where Pierre de Bourdeilles did his writing. The abbey was founded by Charlemagne, and has been updated down the centuries. The little town is a delightful spot, and contains two excellent restaurants, the Chabrol and L'Auberge. One for lunch and one for dinner make a visit to Brantôme a gastronomic experience.

North of Brantôme lies the pleasant little town of Nontron, somewhat overshadowed by the charm of the two towns to the south, but very well worth a visit, standing as it does on a beetling ravine and a good centre for touring the northern marches of the Dordogne.

From Nontron, heading south towards the river, the road runs along a valley past Aubeterre and La Roche Chalais to the town of Coutras.

At Coutras in 1588 Henry of Navarre, later Henry IV of France, fought a decisive engagement against the army of the Catholic League, under their commander, the Duc de Joyeuse.

Henry was a strange mixture, a fine soldier, a great consumer of women, fickle, irresponsible, and dynamic. A typical Bourbon in fact. The Wars of Religion in France at this time had settled to one long engagement between the Holy Catholic League, led by Henry, Duc du Guise, nominally acting for King Henry III of Valois, and against the King's heir, the leader of the Huguenots, Henry of Navarre. This 'War of the Three Henrys' as it was called, had been tearing France apart, and at Coutras the Catholic field army under Joyeuse thought they had the Huguenots in the net, and could finish the war at one blow. They could not have been more wrong. Henry's cannon tore huge gaps in the ranks of the League, and a cavalry charge broke them to pieces. In less than one hour the battle was over, and Henry master of the field.

The Duc de Joyeuse had been unwise enough to order his men, before the battle, to take no prisoners. Surrounded, he threw down his sword crying. 'My ransom is a hundred thousand crowns', but nobody wanted his money, and someone shot him through the head. This victory, which should have put Henry in an unassailable position, rewarded him not at all. That night, leaving his army to head back to its base in Béarn, he went with a few followers to lay the captured League standards at the feet of his current mistress, La Belle Corisande. Henry really was a typical Bourbon, one of that family about whom, it was said later, that they had learned nothing and forgotten nothing. Henry would have made an excellent politician. He could make statesmanlike remarks and gain great credit for his integrity, and then do precisely the opposite, and somehow justify it.

When it was pointed out that the one great stumbling block to his being declared the heir to Henry III was his Protestant faith, he replied that a man's religion was not to be taken on and off like a shirt. Protestant Europe thrilled, for that was it, exactly. That done and credit gained, Henry then remarked that, after all, Paris was worth a Mass, became Catholic, and was duly crowned Henry IV. To be fair, he did, shortly after his coronation, pass the Edict of Nantes, which granted religious toleration throughout France, so perhaps his great heart, was, after all, in the right place.

From Coutras, the road takes us away, back along the valley of the Isle and up, once again, to Périgueux.

CHAPTER V

Along the Dordogne—Libourne to Bergerac

Libourne stands on the north bank of the Dordogne, at the point where it is joined by the Isle, about twenty miles from Bordeaux by road and some fifty miles from the point where the Dordogne joins up with the Garonne. Directly across the river from Libourne the traveller enters the wine growing country on the peninsula that lies between the two rivers and called therefore Entre-deux-mers.

Libourne itself was founded by an Englishman, Roger de Libourne, who was Seneschal of Gascony. It still has some of the medieval fortifications, notably the towers by the Grand Port. Libourne is a good shopping centre and a good base for exploring the wine country to the east, or across the river in Entre-deux-mers. The rivers are tidal here, with a rise of about 10 feet.

The main town in these parts is of course Bordeaux, which has a population of nearly half a million and is a thriving industrial centre. Bordeaux lies outside the scope of this book, but as it owes its development largely to the produce of the Dordogne and Libournaise hinterland, it cannot be entirely neglected.

Bordeaux is a very ancient city which really flowered under the rule of the Dukes of Aquitaine. When Eleanor married Henry II, the export of wine to England, which had already begun, then flourished, and has continued to the present day. The prosperity of Bordeaux was founded on the wine drawn from the vineyards through which we shall now travel.

Libourne makes a good base for this purpose and has an adequate number of hotels at all prices, situated near the railway station. The Hotel Negrier is a good spot to stay, but the restaurant is marred by the fact that they permit dogs in it too. No meal is improved by barking and snarling underfoot. A dog under the next

The towers at Libourne

64

table whiled away the time until its owners had finished eating by tearing up the carpet, which was some consolation. Any restaurant that permits dogs deserves to have the carpets ruined. Indeed the French tolerance of dogs in close proximity to their food is, for a nation so fussy about good food, really quite incredible. The next morning, buying my lunch in a *charcuterie*, I saw a dog wearing a happy expression and blissfully licking a ham! Had it been *biting* it, I would not have minded so much.

Leaving Libourne we take the road east for a few kilometres, and then turn north for St. Emilion.

There was a Gaulish Oppidum, or hill fort, at St. Emilion 2,000 years ago, and there are still traces of prehistoric, Gallic, and Roman occupation. In the eighth century St. Emilion, an Anchorite monk, had his cell here, and founded a small hermitage, around which the beginnings of the present town began to form.

St. Emilion gained its charter from King John, or as the French call him Jean Sans-Terre, John Lackland, in 1199. At the same time he appointed the *Jurade*, a body of twenty-four men good and true, and charged them with the task, not only of looking after the town and the townspeople, but maintaining the standards and quality of the local wine. Successive kings, French and English, have confirmed these rights and duties, and the *Jurade* still rule to this day.

St. Emilion is full of attractions, not least the crumbling, honeysuckle-covered walls around the moat. Inside the walls lies a huge monolithic church hollowed out of the living rock, and crowned by a medieval steeple. The cloisters of the Collegiate church, part of which is now occupied by the local Syndicat d'Initiative or Tourist Office, has to be visited. Apart from the fine medieval setting, it contains an enormous wine press and various other interesting implements connected with the cultivation of the grape. On the opposite hill lies the twelfth century Château du Roi, which once was the only entrance through the walls, and from which, in a good year, the vintage is proclaimed by the *Jurade*. Unchanged, the limestone rocks of St. Emilion have been hollowed out to serve as wine cellars and here in the cool dark, the rich clarets of the region can mature.

The word 'claret' comes from the French *clairet*, which roughly means clear, or light, and the wines are so called because in the Middle Ages they were found to be lighter both in colour and effect

The monolithic church at St. Emilion

Vineyards near St. Emilion

than the richer growths of Burgundy or the South. There are over 500 square miles of claret vineyard to the east of Bordeaux, and they produce annually about 100 million gallons of wine, which is still not enough to go round, so great and growing is the demand for fine wines. Not all this wine is of the same quality, and those of St. Emilion are what are called Burgeois growths, which nevertheless means that they are very fine wines indeed to the average palate.

There are some 10 square miles of vineyards in the area of St. Emilion, and from the town itself there are vineyards in all directions, as far as the eye can see. The town would be a good centre for a walking tour of the local vineyards, for little paths wind everywhere among them and most of the wine producers are happy to welcome visitors, both to sample their wine and buy a bottle to take away.

67

It is noticeable that many of the vines have a rose bush or flowers planted at the end of each row. This certainly breaks up the otherwise monotonous green of the vines, but is of course there to assist in the pollination of the vine. Presumably even an industrious bee can get bored with vine pollen, and, who knows, perhaps it has the same effect on bees as wine has on people. Maybe the bees have to drone back to the hive and sleep it off in the afternoon. Apart from the beneficial effect the rose has on the vine and the bee, the bushes and their scent make a fine walk in a warm summer evening. The vines flower in June, and the grapes are ready to be picked about three months later, when the fields are a maze of busy pickers all hopeful that this will be not just a good year, but a great year, and produce a claret to remember.

From St. Emilion there are various roads down to the river, and so to the east, but pursuing the policy of keeping off the main roads where possible, one can weave through the various vineyards, and inspect their 'château' in passing. All Bordeaux wines, red or white, are 'Château' something, from the lordly Château Lafite, to the ordinary château plonk. Some of the houses of the proprietors do indeed look like châteaux, but others are just large farmhouses. But this is understandable; a bottle of Farmhouse '54 would not be the same thing at all.

Down by the river bank lies the small town of Castillon-la-Bataille. The battle in question took place in April 1453, and was the final battle of the Hundred Years War.

The site of the battle lies outside the town on the plain to the left, off the road to Ste. Foy. A monument marks the spot, an obelisk to the French and their generals, Jean Burau, who commanded the artillery and the Breton, Count de Penthièvre, who commanded the *gens d'ordonnance*.

Castillon saw, at last, the eclipse of the English archer. For nearly 150 years, his harrow-shaped ranks standing quietly on a hillside, behind a hedge of stakes, had struck dispair into his enemies, but the French would not play that game any more, and once his enemies refused to advance into the arrow storm, the archer's supremacy disappeared.

It is curious how the English soldier prefers to fight a defensive battle. From Senlac to Waterloo his greatest victories, often against odds, were when he turned at bay and forced the enemy to attack him. Once firmly established, English infantry could not be easily dislodged and an enemy would wreck his army against their stubborn lines. The French had success in battle during the Hundred Years War, usually when they took the English by surprise, or on the march, and charged before the archers could plant their stakes, but it took three generations for them to revise their tactics and force the English on to the offensive. The English general, John Talbot, 'great marshal to Henry VI, of all his wars within the realm of the French', was forced to lead his archers on an assault on the entrenched French who had artillery, and the result was a disaster. In the battle fell the flower of the English infantry, the only field army they had was totally destroyed, and worst of all Talbot was killed, and he was irreplaceable. Talbot's son, young John, was killed in the first assault on the French position and when his father heard the news he turned back from the rout and sought his own death among his enemies, a wasted end for a man who, as Shakespeare put it, was 'England's glory, Gallia's wonder'. There is a monument to Talbot on the river bank nearby.

The next stop on the road east is the little hamlet of Montcaret-Tête-Noir, a name to conjure with in the fourteenth century. Geoffrey Tête-Noir was the most notorious, and most successful, captain of *routiers*, in the French wars, and from his base at Montcaret he could demand ransom and tribute from travellers on their way to Bordeaux, whether they travelled by road or by river. Montcaret today has a fine old church, and some Roman mosaics. It also has, more usefully at lunchtime, the Auberge de Pierre, opposite the church, where the menu offered a five-course meal including wine for 13 francs, which at present is about £1.25. This seemed too good to miss, and proved excellent, sending me on my way rejoicing. Geoffrey Tête-Noir would rotate in his grave if he knew that any traveller to his town got off so lightly.

The small village of St. Michel de Montaigne north-west of Montcaret, is on a hill dominated by an enormous château. The village is a small, quiet place, an unlikely home for a man whose reputation has brought us here, a reputation that has girdled the world and spanned four centuries.

Michel de Eyquem Montaigne was born in 1533, the son of a prosperous local knight, Pierre Eyquem, of Bordeaux and

Portrait of Michel de Montaigne

Montaigne. Montaigne's mother was a Spanish Jewess, Antoinette de Lopez, and since the Jewish religion descends through the mother, he was technically a Jew. It is an academic point for Montaigne was baptised a Catholic like his forefathers, and remained one all his life. He did, however, inherit from his mother the Jewish love of literature and the arts.

He was the eldest of eight children, and at sixteen went to the University of Toulouse where he read law and philosophy. On coming down, in 1554, he opened a legal practice in Périgueux, at the same time as his father became Mayor of Bordeaux, to which town Montaigne transferred his practice in 1557. This was during the early Wars of Religion, and as they raged across the south, Catholic Bordeaux became the centre for the persecution of the Huguenots, who in turn were harassing the surrounding countryside on which the trade of the port depended.

In 1565 Montaigne got married, choosing a rich heiress, and when his father died three years later, Montaigne found himself a wealthy man, with lands and property both in Bordeaux and Montaigne. He had six children, all but one of which died before him, and he died at his home in Montaigne in 1592, at the age of fifty-nine.

During his lifetime he gained a great reputation for his tolerance, his judgement, and his literary skill. His great contribution to the world of letters was in his invention of the essay as a literary form.

The word essay comes from the French *essai*, which really means test or trial. In his essay, Montaigne submits his beliefs and ideas to tests of self examination and his books of essays are a continuous test of his attitude to the world and its beliefs. He is nothing if not frank, and the essays reveal a critical style which still entertains us today.

Montaigne was a sceptic, 'Call no man happy until he is dead' was one of his sayings. 'Although we sit in the highest throne in the world we still sit on our own tail' was another. He had his pen in his hand, his eye on society, and his tongue in his cheek, not a bad position from which to survey a reeling world. Montaigne would have said he was a realist.

With his many talents, Montaigne was much sought after as a councillor. He became Mayor of Bordeaux and a confidant of Henry of Navarre. Henry, laden with the standards of Coutras, stopped at Montaigne on his way to visit Corisande. Had Montaigne lived long after Henry was crowned, the King would have forced him to become the Chancellor of France.

Montaigne could have been anything he wished, but he was without ambition and preferred to stay at home in the Dordogne and write. The only strong influence on his life was his close friend, Etienne de la Boetie. The two men took to each other on first meeting, and their friendship lasted until la Boetie's death, a loss from which Montaigne never quite recovered. There are, truly, few signs of any other person or belief influencing Montaigne. In an age torn by conflicting religions and political beliefs, he remained firmly on the side of moderation and tolerance.

Indeed, it is this and his cheerful scepticism that makes him such a relief. Through history one hears of people scourged and driven by passionate beliefs, often based on the most sketchy facts or reasoning. How refreshing to meet someone who not only viewed the whole world with total disregard, but continued to do so when it was greatly to his material advantage to do otherwise. He was an adequate Mayor of Bordeaux, but at that level he stopped. He retired at every opportunity to a tower in his castle at Montaigne and there he wrote.

The Château of Montaigne is not the one we see there today. That was destroyed by fire, though luckily Montaigne's tower survived, and is incorporated in the present building.

Here we can still see the rooms in which Montaigne lived and worked, the beams covered with sayings from his own favourite writers, Plutarch and Seneca. He could push back his chair and gaze up at these sayings and, no doubt, spend hours like that, or looking out from his tower across the valley vineyards of the Dordogne.

He describes the tower in his writings, 'My tower has a chapel on the ground floor, and my bedroom on the second. On the third is my library, which is circular in shape, and being rounded it shows me all my books at once, arranged on five tiers of shelves. From this room, I have open views, and sixteen clear paces to exercise. This is my throne and here I rule absolutely, reserving this one corner from all society.'

He was a lucky man to have such a retreat, and we, too, are lucky that so much remains to remind us of a man, who, from a wealth

Michel de Montaigne's tower

73

of opportunity had the wisdom to know the value of a little peace and quiet.

Now down towards the Dordogne, and across the river to the village of Pessac, which has a most unusual church.

The road to Ste. Foy la Grande follows the south bank closely and this seems a good opportunity to take another look at the river as we travel away from the road. Very little of the river is visible, but the church at Pessac is worth a look, for it is the most jumbled structure, with a small Byzantine style belfry graced by two large bells.

Ste. Foy lies on the south bank of the Dordogne at a point where two bridges cross the river. Indeed, one of the factors that make travelling in the Dordogne so enjoyable is that there are plenty of bridges, and one can cross from one side to the other with comparative ease. The nicest part of Ste. Foy is the river bank, which is, as usual, crowded with fishermen. I have noticed that French fishermen never seem to catch anything, and stand there for hours clutching their heavy poles (they are far too heavy to be called rods) and go home at last empty handed. This particular evening I decided to ask them if they had caught anything, and not one, out of fifteen, had had a bite. And yet there are plenty of fish in the river and they jump in the evening up among the swifts and swallows flighting after the low flies.

Ste. Foy was held for the Protestants during the Wars of Religion, and was largely destroyed in the years of incessant warfare. Originally, it was a *bastide*, built as a fortified town in the fourteenth century, but the fighting of the sixteenth century has destroyed much of that graceful medieval feeling and only the straightness of the streets and the connecting alleyways, typical of a *bastide* give a link to the first foundation.

Ste. Foy possesses two pleasant hotels, the Boule d'Or and the Cheval Blanc, both of which have good, reasonable accommodation and adequate restaurants. It is, therefore, a good place to stop and prepare for further exploration up the river, and is for that reason a good place to close this chapter.

CHAPTER VI

Into the Bastide Country

Bergerac marks a change in the Dordogne, and the river valley, as we journey upstream. Above Bergerac the hills edge down from the north and reach across the river past Couze, still rising up until they topple over into the valley of the Dordogne's southern sister, the Lot.

Bergerac itself, where we start this section of our travels is the largest town in the central Dordogne and, being a focus of road and rail traffic, is a well-developed commercial centre. In spite of this it exercises considerable charm, and has an enterprising history drawn more from fiction than reality, but none the less entertaining for all that.

Bergerac is of course the birthplace of Rostand's tragic hero, that peerless swordsman and silent lover, the man with the fatal nose, Cyrano de Bergerac.

Cyrano, of course, never existed, but he was an archetypal Gascon, one of those gallant soldiers, 'whose only fortune was a sword, and a few barren acres to starve on', who flocked into the armies of the Sun King, and carved such a place for themselves in French history. D'Artagnan, who actually did exist, and was indeed a captain of the musketeers, is another Gascon and one whose colourful career is well known to Englishmen through the fictional pages of Alexandre Dumas. The people of the Dordogne are Gascons. Never mind precise geographical considerations, they are Gascons in the same way that many Londoners far from the sound of Bow Bells claim to be cockney. And the Dordogne was, for much of history, in Gascony, or Guinne, or Guyenne or Aquitaine, a variety of names that all add up to much the same thing.

Bergerac, like Ste. Foy, was a Huguenot town, and was largely destroyed in the Wars of Religion, with the exception of the old church of St. Jacques, near the river, which survived this period.

75

After the revocation of the Edict of Nantes in 1685, most of the population fled abroad and the town went into decline. It was saved from extinction by the introduction of tobacco, which, it was discovered, would grow well in the local countryside.

Bergerac is the major centre in France for the growing and processing of tobacco and has a Museum of Tobacco which traces the development of the trade from the sixteenth century. Bergerac is also a fine shopping centre, and the principal market town for the local agriculture, which includes the growing of that other staple, the fine red wines of Bergerac. Over the river, heading towards the *bastide* country, the road runs through more vineyards, but these produce the local white wine, Monbazillac. Personally, I do not care for Monbazillac, and find it too sweet, but it is *the* wine of the Dordogne, and if you ask simply for a glass of wine, Monbazillac is what you will be offered. A drier, white wine is from Duras in the Libournaise and Château Duras is a very palatable dry, white wine.

The village of Monbazillac has the usual imposing château, built about 1550. There are wonderful views from the grounds of the château, back over the Dordogne valley towards Bergerac, and for a more sweeping panorama the traveller can visit the Moulin de Malfourat, only a few kilometres away, as we head back to the main road and our first *bastide*, Eymet.

The word *bastide* comes from the French *bastir*, to build. From about the middle of the thirteenth century, both English and French kings sought to consolidate their holdings in the south-west by constructing a series of fortified towns. They discovered that simply to stud a land with castles and garrison them with soldiers was not enough. If a land was to survive as anything other than a desert then it must be supplied by an industrious civil population, who could not maintain themselves on the march without protection from those scourges of the Middle Ages, the *routiers*. By the fourteenth century the *routiers* had got themselves organised, and in Free Companies lived off the land and its inhabitants. They called themselves the *Tard-Venus*, the Late Comers, and in peace or war they made the land a living hell. Some Free Companies were very large. When the English captain John Hawkwood took his White Company to Italy, it is recorded that he had over 200 mounted men at arms and 1,000 English archers. No wonder his arrival in Italy proved so decisive in the wars between the city states.

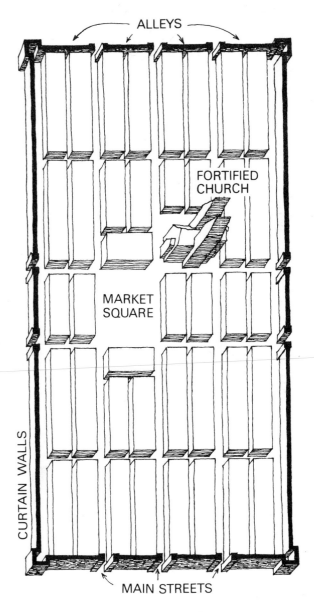

Plan of a bastide

77

From about 1250 then, *bastides* began to appear, small fortified towns in which the inhabitants enjoyed many freedoms for going there, from taxation, for example, and as a bonus were frequently given holdings outside the walls, and the town was also given a charter for a market.

Bastides were usually built on the same lines, a rectangle with outside walls, each street running at right angles to the next, and with narrow alleys or *canyiou*, linking up each main street. In the centre was a covered market hall, and the church was usually fortified as a last refuge if the defences were overwhelmed.

A typical *bastide* looked like the diagram on page 77.

The rectangular blocks of houses could each be defended in turn, while the alleys could be used for outflanking movements or retreats, and were too narrow to enable a mounted knight to use his weapons. Another typical feature of the *bastide*, and one which,

Cornieres at Eymet

happily, remains in use to this day, were the *cornières*, or arches which formed the lower storey of the houses in the central square. Under these arches the merchant could have his shop and display his wares, and they are still in use for the same purpose today, the shopkeeper living upstairs, over the store.

Bastides were built all over the south-west, but the most attractive are in the south of the Department of the Dordogne, in the hilly country overlooking the Lot.

Eymet, south of Bergerac, was a French *bastide*, and is still in an excellent condition, with the arcades decorating the main square, and a medieval castle, now somewhat in ruins, just by the church. Near this château is the municipal 'camping'. There are many camp-sites in the Dordogne, and while some are better than others, all are very good. The one at Eymet is typical, and as a guide to the rest is worth describing. Situated on a large, tree-lined lawn, it

Issigeac

79

has a resident manager, showers, lavatories, sinks for washing clothes, swings, and a sand pit for smaller children. It is, at the most, two minutes from the centre of town and costs, for full use of the facilities, 2 francs per person per day. A family of four could stay there for about 75p a day, and with everything in excellent order, this does seem the most excellent value. Not that the hotels in the town are expensive. At the Hôtel du Château, in the Rue de Cruvent, for example, a night stop including dinner and wine will cost about £3. Rural France need not be expensive, and whatever it costs, the traveller usually gets excellent value for money. These prices are those that apply in mid-1974, and over the years that this book will stay in print, one will need to calculate for increases, but I believe that the principle of value for money will hold good for many years ahead.

East of Eymet lies the picturesque little town of Issigeac. Issigeac is not a *bastide*, but is such a lovely little place that no tour of the Southern Dordogne should leave it out. The road to Issigeac is a delightful run, and so beautiful is the countryside that simply to stay in the car is impossible. A walk across a meadow is a sheer delight in the early morning, for apart from the host of blue, red, and yellow flowers, clouds of butterflies of all colours start up from the grass and flutter about, knee high, as you walk. The country, has, overall, every appearance of a march. A number of hills are crowned with watchtowers, and the farms are clustered tightly on their hilltops, the older ones bearing every sign of defensive construction. This country forms part of the so called Périgord Noir, lying south and east of Périgueux, and straddling the river west of the Vézère valley.

From Issigeac we head out of the Dordogne to visit another French *bastide*, Villeréal. The road offers some wonderful views, and more signs of fortification. Maybe, in their time, the castles and towers of the medieval lord were regarded with just the same disgust as we view the office blocks of the captains of industry today. However, I wonder if in eight centuries they will still stand, and blend so well into the landscape. Somehow, I doubt it. Villeréal stands on the little river Dropt, a pleasant stream, and is a pleasant little town, built in 1265 by Alphonse de Poitiers, the brother of St. Louis, in an attempt to prevent further advances to the north

by the English. Villeréal fell to the English during the Hundred
Years War, and remained in their hands for many years.

The church and covered market were also built by Alphonse de
Poitiers, and the walls of the church are immensely thick and were
sturdy enough to withstand the cannon of the Huguenot when they
attacked the town in 1572, although the outer façade of the church
suffered considerably. Seen in the sunlight, with vines trailing down
the walls of the golden stone houses and hovering over the geraniums, Villeréal is a lovely spot, and it lies, not in the Dordogne, but
in the Department of Lot-et-Garonne.

A cycle would be an excellent way to travel around the *bastide*
country for the little towns are each within a couple of days' ride
of each other, and the quiet passage of a bicycle seems very suited
to this mellow landscape.

Along the road from Villeréal to Monpazier, I met my first
shepherdess, supposedly a memorable encounter in any man's life,
and she turned out to be a large and amiable lady of a certain age,
strolling along with some 200 happy nibbling sheep.

A turning on the right off this road takes one to the mighty château
of Biron. What a place! Many castles in the Dordogne are big,
some are large, like Hautefort for example, but Biron is vast. The
castles of the Dordogne were not built as pretty toys, or to give
credence to newly won nobility, but for war, and for defence in
time of war, to nail down an uncertain frontier in the interest of the
lord, and the tall, thick, crenellated walls gave ample proof that, in
their day, before the coming of artillery, and even afterwards, they
were formidable fortresses.

Biron, the village as well as the castle, is a dream. The church
which stands below the walls of the castle is a beautiful building,
with a Renaissance house built into one side, and it is so well
matched and finely formed that one could sit and gaze at it for
hours.

The castle stands on a mound which is itself on the top of a small
hill. It was constructed over the centuries, but the bulk of the construction dates from the sixteenth century, and the most attractive
feature is the way you get in. The visitor climbs up a steep ramp,
so little used that grass grows quite thickly in the verges. At the top
you are confronted by a massive door, the sort that it would seem
natural to beat on with the butt of a lance. Beside the door hangs

In the courtyard at Biron

a chain which, when pulled, clangs a large bell suspended overhead.

The head of the châtelaine appears over the battlements; having seen who it is, she descends to open the door with much dragging of bolts and rattling of chain—just as most travellers have entered the castle in the past, and so much nicer than a turnstile and a ticket desk. Inside, the castle is wonderful. The views from the walls are breathtaking, and the castle has everything a castle should have: a dungeon, ramps and battlements, a huge kitchen, and a wonderful chapel with the effigies of some of the previous owners.

Biron was, in the sixteenth century, the home of Charles de Gontaut, soldier, and intimate, like his father before him, of Henry of Navarre. When Henry came to the French throne as Henry IV, he richly rewarded his old comrade in arms, whom he created admiral and later Marshal of France, and awarded him the Barony of Biron, and the governship of Bordeaux. But de Gontaut was one of those people who felt that even half of Henry's kingdom would not be enough, since he had helped the King gain all of it. He plotted to betray the King, and divide the kingdom. When his plot was discovered, Henry forgave de Gontaut, and returned him his possessions, only to be betrayed again by another plot. Henry offered to pardon de Gontaut yet again, if he would kneel and ask forgiveness, but his proud servant refused. Having no option, the King ordered his execution and he was beheaded outside the Bastille in 1602. Curiously enough, his father also lost his head, struck off in battle by a cannon-ball.

Biron is a wonderful castle, and a must for any visitor to the Dordogne. It does not, in fact, receive many visitors. In an average year, only some 5,000 people visit it, and the castle is large enough to absorb that many in a single day. The day I went there, I had the place completely to myself. On leaving the castle and returning to my car, I found it occupied by a large and truculent hornet, which refused all invitations to leave. Finally a chase in and out of all doors, round the back seat and front, left my copy of the Michelin Green Guide and myself in a decidedly frayed condition, at which point the hornet, after droning round the car a few times to show who was master, took off through the sliding roof, which thereafter remained tightly shut at every halt.

The next halt is the beautiful *bastide* of Monpazier, perhaps the most beautiful of all the southern *bastides*. Monpazier was an early

Arches in Monpazier

bastide, founded by the order of the English King, Edward I, in 1267. His seneschal in these parts was one Pierre de Gontaut, an ancestor of Marshal Biron, who oversaw the construction of the town, which changed hands several times during the Hundred Years War. Monpazier has all the finest features of the *bastide*, a fine covered market, a fortified church, though reconstructed in the mid-sixteenth century, and the usual alleyways and arcades. Monpazier is in some danger of becoming chic. Already some of the arcades have become the sites of fashionable little shops, but the town has enough charm to beat off the forces of commercialism for a good few years yet.

Villefranche-du-Périgord, the next *bastide* in our tour, lies southeast of Monpazier, and is yet another beautiful little town, in the typical *bastide* fashion, with a most splendid covered market, a fine church and more recently an excellent hotel and restaurant overlooking the valley of the Lemance.

Villefranche, as the name implies, is a French *bastide*, built, once again, by Alphonse de Poitiers in about 1270, and is a pleasant town and something of a leisure centre, with riding, tennis, swimming, and cycling all catered for and being energetically enjoyed by crowds of youngsters, seemingly quite unaffected by the dazzling sunlight and the heat.

The road north, to further *bastides* and back to the Dordogne, takes one to the little village of Siorac, which, apart from an excellent camping site on the very banks of the river, contains the wonderful little Auberge de La Petite Reine, a Logis de France, with a fine dining room, and, very welcome in the heat of the day, a swimming pool.

At Siorac one can turn west to visit the Cistercian monastery at Cadouin, where the story of the Holy Shroud is an object lesson in advisability of leaving well alone.

The possession of relics was one of the passions of ecclesiastical foundations in the Middle Ages, and some time after the First Crusade, in the early years of the twelfth century, the monastery of Cadouin acquired a piece of linen that had reputedly wrapped the head of Christ after the crucifixion.

Possession of such a relic brought fame and great wealth to the monastery for pilgrims rich and poor, humbled and mighty, came from all Christendom to visit the shrine of the Shroud. This con-

Hotel du Commerce in Villefranche

The abbey at Cadouin

tinued until the early years of the nineteenth century, when a monk with more learning than brains, decided to have the shroud examined by experts, and they not only dated it at about AD 1100, but stated that the embroidery on the hem was Arabic. Within months the secret was out, and the pilgrimages to Cadouin stopped. Today Cadouin is a quiet place with no crowds waiting patiently before the great doors of the Romanesque abbey, but one imagines that when the curious monk came up for his next penitential scourging, his brother monks laid on the strokes with a particular will.

Near Cadouin lies the English *bastide* of Beaumont, built at the end of the thirteenth century, and still retaining, apart from the visual *bastide* features, most of the original fortifications.

Beaumont is a riot of flowers, in particular those pots of dark geraniums that are set off so beautifully by the grey gold of the sunlit walls. Beaumont has two lines of walls, the outer carrying

Fortified church at Beaumont

the narrow ring road at its foot, and the inner offering a wide grassy footpath for a circular tour of the town. It has a fine church inhabited by squadrons of swooping swifts, swallows, and martins, which nest in the high corners of the huge building.

The road from Beaumont back to the Dordogne takes one beside the little river Couze, a noted trout stream, and past the towers and pinnacles of the castle of Bannes. Bannes is a fairytale castle, the type that the princess always has in the story-books, and set on green wooded hills it seems to epitomise the legends of chivalry and romance.

Over the Dordogne at Couze and travelling east, brings us to Lalinde, also a *bastide*, but one which, after some industrialisation, bears little sign of it. Lalinde does, however, contain the fine and reasonable Hôtel du Château, standing right on the banks of the sparkling Dordogne and appearing at first glance to be constructed mainly of ivy. Dinner on the terrace by the river there makes a perfect ending to the day.

CHAPTER VII

Prehistory in the Vézère Valley

The study of prehistory is a comparatively new branch of archaeology. The word 'prehistory' itself was only coined in 1851, and needs some definition. Essentially prehistory records the history of man in those ages before history was, or could be, written down. In the purest sense, all man's past, from yesterday to the dawn of time, is history, whether recorded on papyrus or stone, or simply deduced from the artefacts and rubbish that history left behind.

Prehistory needed a finer definition than this, because, certainly in the seventeenth and eighteenth centuries, any idea of man's history being unwritten would have been regarded as heretical, or patently absurd, for all men knew that man's history had been carefully recorded from before Creation in the pages of the Old Testament.

The theological student, and any traveller who has spent years of his life in hotel bedrooms with nothing to read but the Gideon Bible, becomes at least an amateur theologian and can readily accept that, by reading the Old Testament, noting the longevity of the characters and their various begattings, the length of time since man's arrival can be easily calculated. Dr. John Lightfoot, Vice-Chancellor of Cambridge University, did just that in 1642, and came up with the statement: 'Man was created by the Trinity on 23rd October 4004 BC at nine o'clock in the morning.'

This statement was not really challenged for the next 150 years, in spite of the expansion of man's knowledge. It was possible to fit Roman, Greek, and Persian empires into a past of nearly 6,000 years. And even Stonehenge or Carnac, or the finds of the early archaeologists that did not seem to fit any known epoch, failed to distort the tacit acceptance of man's divine origin. It was the geologists who brought prehistory into the light. In their study of the earth's strata, a study very fashionable in the eighteenth century, a continuous stream of curious objects was discovered, some, animal-like fossils and the bones of strange beasts, others, like stone axes, and flint arrowheads, clearly of human origin. That man had an early ancestor who lived in caves and hunted his prey with stone weapons became accepted. Then, in 1816, a Dane, Rasmus Nyerup first defined the three historical ages of man, and named them the Stone, Bronze and Iron Ages.

The Three Age System, as it is called, although it seems very simple and obvious to us now, made a great impact at the time, and has indeed endured as the basis for all age stratification in archaeology. It soon became apparent that the Stone Age had lasted a lot longer than the other two, and the Stone Age itself came to be subdivided into the Old Stone Age, or Palaeolithic, the Middle, or Mesolithic, and the New, or Neolithic. It also became clear that of these three subdivisions, the Palaeolithic had been by far the longest, and it in turn needed sub-dividing.

Modern man does not need to be told that the pace of life is getting quicker; although expressed in thousands, and tens of thousands of years, that is what has been happening since man first appeared on the earth's crust, probably about 1 million years ago. Each age, and sub-age has been shorter than the previous one.

The earliest man we have heard of so far lived about 150,000 years ago, and from the discovery of his remains at Neanderthal, near Düsseldorf, we call him Neanderthal Man. He lived in the Middle Palaeolithic period, was a cave dweller and used stone and flint weapons. Neanderthal Man stayed around for a long time, gradually evolving, and one of the places where he has left many traces of his development is along the valley of the river Vézère, in the Dordogne. Neanderthal Man developed what is known as the Mousterian culture, based on hunting and cave-dwelling.

The Dordogne was below the limit of the advancing ice in the last Ice Age, and in the caves and hollows of the limestone cliffs early man could build shelters and survive.

As a result of these settlements, the Dordogne has made a significant contribution to the study of prehistory, and following the practice of naming discoveries after the place in which they are found, the region has contributed Mousterian, Cro-Magnon and Magdalenian Man to our knowledge of the human species.

Cro-magon man at Les Eyzies

About 60,000 years ago, *homo sapiens* replaced Neanderthal Man, living in groups in caves, working in stone. A magnificent example of Mousterian Man is found at the Roche St. Christophe near La Moustier and Cro-Magnon Man made his debut in a cave above Les Eyzies. Cro-Magnon Man, who appeared about 40,000 years ago, is a fairly advanced example of the human race, and far removed from the ape-like Neanderthal. Magdalenian Man, who dates from the Upper Palaeolithic, about 20,000–30,000 years ago, was named from the discovery made at La Madeleine near Tusac, by the Vézère, in 1863. It was Magdalenian Man who executed the world famous wall paintings at Lascaux, about 30,000 years ago. It should be pointed out that all these dates are very general, and, as dating techniques are revised, become changeable, but as steps in man's development, they are valid.

The whole area of the Vézère is a prehistoric site. Cliff dwellings, grottoes, grave pits, all abound, and archaeologists are still delving ever deeper into the hills of the region, probing under the crust to see what fresh evidence can be discovered.

The Vézère joins the Dordogne at Limeuil, and the road follows the winding course of the Vézère, on one bank or another, all the way up to Montignac. Prehistoric sites lie on either side of the road, which is flanked by steep limestone cliffs, which, you quickly notice, contain holes and caves obviously not of natural origin. Past Le Bugue, and you enter the town of Les Eyzies de Tayac, sometime home of Cro-Magnon Man.

Cro-Magnon Man was discovered here in 1865, by some work-men digging the road. They found a rock shelter containing the skeletons of a whole family, two adults and three children, who were eventually classified as from the Upper Palaeolithic, and called Cro-Magnon. The Cro-Magnon Hotel now stands on the site of this discovery.

Above the hotel, built into an old prehistoric cave shelter and the remains of a medieval castle, is the National Museum of Prehistory, at which any tour of the valley ought to start. This provides the visitor, although only in French, with full information on the development of man. Outside the Museum stands a huge statue, supposedly of Cro-Magnon Man himself. He appears as a huge, bewildered, shambling brute, quite unlike the actual Cro-Magnon who, as his skull inside the Museum indicated, was of modern

Cliff dwellings of prehistoric man at St. Christophe

appearance, and quite a handsome creature. Another curious site at Les Eyzies is the Roc de La Peine, a cliff eroded by wind and water which hangs out over the road on the outskirts of the town.

I cannot say that I really care for present day Les Eyzies. It is organised to cope with the visitor, and although a pleasant town with good hotels, camping and restaurants, it gives one no feel for what the valley or life in it must have been like for prehistoric man.

Fortunately, further up the road, at Le Moustier, on the Roque St. Christophe, you get a very good idea indeed. Well wooded, the high cliffs of St. Christophe have a timeless air, and a tour of the prehistoric cave dwellings, hollowed out high in the cliffs is an enlightening experience.

The prehistoric village, for that is what it is, is on five levels, reaching a total height of almost 300 feet. The cliff drops sheer away to the Vézère, and the tour should not be attempted by anyone who suffers from vertigo. Here you can see the caves where prehistoric man lived, the recesses for water, the niches for fires, the places where animals were tethered, and the painfully hacked out staircases that gave him access from one level to another. This cave village must have been impregnable to anything but starvation, and here, safe from the attacks of wild men and wilder beasts, early man survived.

The Roque was a fortress again in the Middle Ages, and was occupied by bandits who ravaged the surrounding countryside until the Lord of Limeuil captured the place in 1400, and hanged everyone who survived.

The Roque is quite alarming enough to climb in peacetime, and anyone wishing to see the sights should have a head for heights. On a recent visit my party was joined by a complaining middle-aged lady, who was accompanied by a large and cowardly Dalmatian dog. This animal had no aptitude for heights and got steadily more miserable as it was dragged higher until, on the fifth level, it lay down howling and refused to move. Discord then arose between the lady and the rest of the group, which was resolved by the suggestion that if she would find her own way down, the men in the party would take turns to carry the dog. The lady agreed provided that great care was taken with the Dalmatian. Descending a sheer cliff by rickety stairs and slippery steps, while clutching a large, yowling, wriggling hound, is not everyone's idea of good fun, and the lady and her pet shared the unique distinction of being cursed in five languages in as many minutes before we reached the bottom.

On the other side of Les Eyzies, and signposted for miles around, lies the Grotto of Le Grand Roc. This is a large cavern, hollowed out of the limey rock by the action of the water over countless centuries.

Wonderful stalagmites and stalactites rise and fall everywhere, and the whole cavern is well lit, to bring out the colours of the crystallised limestone. This cave was located in 1924, and is visited by thousands of people every year, none of whom can suffer from claustrophobia. The Grotto is reached by a low narrow tunnel 40 metres long, and the feeling of thousands of tons of rock brushing your hair is quite oppressive.

Just past Le Grand Roc is a prehistoric site of the Magdalenian period at Laugerie-Busse, while the same road will take you to the Museum of Speleology, or as it is more prosaically known, pot-holing. Here all manner of techniques and discoveries are revealed and, as the region attracts pot-holers from all over the world, it is a popular exhibition. Outside, one can visit the Gorge d'Enfer which has various rock shelters, one of which contains the most wonderful carving of a huge fish, nearly 4 feet long. The Gorge also harbours much wildlife, nightingales nesting on the high cliffs, and the bird-song in the early evening is quite deafening.

Although the prime attraction of the Valley of the Vézère is the prehistoric sites, it has had a long history in more recent times and contains some attractive villages and castles, notably the fortified church at Tayac.

Above Le Bugue lies the pleasant village of Campagne, which has a fine castle built in the fifteenth century, and situated in a small park just beside the road. This is just below the Roches de Lingle, which like the cliffs at Roque St. Christophe, served as a refuge during the Hundred Years War, as also did the cliffs at Tayac just outside Les Eyzies. I find it curious that the existence of prehistoric man could so long have been ignored when successive generations, down to quite recent times, used his caves and shelters and must have passed on the knowledge of their existence from father to son by word of mouth, for centuries. The same consideration holds true in England for monuments such as Stonehenge, although this was attributed to the pagan religion of the Druids. Nevertheless it is extraordinary that scholars can ignore or deny the existence of evidence, which is common knowledge to ordinary simple folk who can see the unusual remains, and because they have always been there, accept them as normal.

The inhabitants of the Vézère valley must, over the centuries, have noticed something unusual, or at least different in their valley, and the place is not that much of a backwater. Nevertheless, it was not until the last 100 years that any major discoveries were made.

The cave at La Mouthe which has some fine wall paintings was not discovered until 1895, Cap Blanc which has some famous carvings, was not discovered until 1909, and Bara Bao, at the lower end of the valley, was not investigated until 1951. The cave of Commarque was not discovered until 1917, and that is actually under the castle there.

The area as one can see, is full of prehistory, and the interested visitor is advised to stay at Les Eyzies, or Montignac, and explore the region thoroughly. Prehistorians and pot-holers flock from all over the world, and their researches are now creeping back up the Dordogne valley towards the still unexplored areas of the Massif Central.

Nevertheless, in spite of a century of exploration by archaeologists, the most famous discovery in the region was made, not by a team of scientists, but by two small boys and a dog. The story has become a classic, but it is worth retelling.

One day in the autumn of 1940, two boys from the town of Montignac went walking with their dog Robot, in the low hills east of the town. Robot put up a rabbit, and disappeared down a hole after it. When he failed to reappear, the boys investigated the spot, and found an entrance clogged by brambles, and the leader, pushing his way through, also disappeared. He fell headlong down a steep slope in the dark, and it took much shouting and some urging before his companion would follow.

When he did, bringing with him a torch, they saw, on the walls, wondrous sights. Great cows and bulls jostled the red deer, and the horses. The boys gazed entranced until the batteries of the torch gave out, when they made their way back to the surface.

At this point someone will want to know about Robot. He was found and lived to a good age.

Cave paintings were no real novelty to the children of Montignac,

A cave painting from Les Eyzies

and it was only in the course of conversation that they mentioned the find to their schoolmaster. He made them take him back, and relocate the entrance, and, with proper light, had the first good look at the astounding sight. This was 1940, and wartime, but the news quickly reached the noted French archaeologist, Abbé Breuil, and broke upon the world.

Lascaux is remarkable. The history of archaeology records no other place like it. The paintings are superb works of genuine, primitive art. The colours are fine and clear, still vivid after 20,000 years, and date from the Upper Palaeolithic period, having the precision and purity of line of fine art. The most striking thing of all is the colour. The great red cattle and the yellow deer are remarkably vivid, and the film of crystal which the walls have sweated have preserved the colours with remarkable clarity. Or rather they did, until 1940. Although it was wartime, people flocked to Lascaux in massive numbers, and although every care was taken, more damage was done to 'the paintings' in the next twenty years than in the previous 20,000. The heat generated by the crowds and the movement of air caused a rapid deterioration in the paintings, and regrettably, the cave was closed to the general public in 1963. Today, only a few visitors are admitted, usually those with special archaeological connections or reasons for visiting the caves. It is always worth applying, and for those with good reason permission is usually granted. Meanwhile there are excellent reproductions on view at the site of the cave, perched on a tree-clad slope, and a trip to the area is a pleasant excursion. It is a pity that such great art must be kept from public view, and perhaps one day a method of preserving the paintings will be found, thus enabling the Beaux Arts to open the cave once more.

From Lascaux, the traveller can choose a number of ways back to the Dordogne, to continue the journey upstream.

One good route lies through Rouffignac, west of Montignac, which has a prehistoric grotto and fine sixteenth century church, which was the only building to escape destruction when the Germans, 'Das Reich' again, burned the village as a reprisal in 1944. Now largely rebuilt, Rouffignac is a pleasant spot set among rolling hills across which it is a short run to Vergt, which was the site of a great battle in the Wars of Religion, and is now famous for strawberries. From there the road south runs past the castles at Gaubertie and Montastruc, and back to Bergerac from which the next leg of our journey begins, up the Dordogne to Domme.

CHAPTER VIII

Along the River—Bergerac to Domme

For the next two chapters, our journey takes us up the Dordogne, from Bergerac to Beaulieu. The river changes greatly in this section, as does the country through which it passes, and this change becomes noticeable as we move east and north towards the Massif Central, and the source of the Dordogne.

On this part of the journey we pass through castle country. For a time it seems as if every rock and hilltop, every cliff and crag is crowned with a fortress, and this is practically true. The middle of the Dordogne is thronged with castles and they give to a naturally beautiful countryside a great air of gaiety and romance.

This, historically speaking, is quite correct, for the very idea of romance, the idea of love, if you like, was introduced to the western world by the lords and ladies of the Languedoc. They cannot have conceived the mischief they were making. Up to the twelfth century, the idea that a man and woman should or ought to love each other as a basis of a happy life together was not merely unthought, but unthinkable. Marriages among those of gentle origin were frequently contracted at birth by the parents, as a basis for a merging of property or to cement an alliance. No woman was expected to love her husband, and the husband was not expected to be faithful to his wife, for what had to be given as a duty could hardly be regarded as a gift. In Languedoc all this was changing, and the fashion of wooing a lady, competing for her favours and falling blindly in love was accepted as one of life's more delightful attractions, but one reserved, be it noted, for married ladies only.

The unmarried ones were kept carefully chaperoned and while they would consider their social life a disaster without a string of gallants serenading them at their window, or wearing their colours in the joust, it went no further.

It is also very unlikely that any knightly swain received physical reward for years of adoration to his chosen lady. But the very idea that a lady of reputation could have an admirer, who broadcast his love and passion, would have given any baron from north of the Loire cause to saddle his warhorse, and look out his heaviest mace. Down south it was all part of the excessively enjoyable pastime of courtly love. Needless to say that gay and enchanting lady, Eleanor of Aquitaine, was a prime mover in this field, and at her father's court at Poitiers she held Courts of Love, at which her ladies and their followers discussed the finer points of romance, and judged each other's skills in the affairs of the heart. It was all very harmless, and although Eleanor reputedly had affairs, notably when she accompanied her husband on the fiasco of the Second Crusade, there is no real proof that she ever went to bed with anyone other than her husband.

Aquitaine, with the bright sunlight, the beautiful countryside, and the clean air, is the place for romance, a land fit for lovers. And in the castles of the Dordogne, a lot of loving, mostly unrequited, did fill up the major part of the day.

From Bergerac, the road runs due east, along the north bank of the river through Lalinde, and on towards Tremolat. At the hamlet of Sauve Boeuf, one can turn right into the north bank of the river and proceed almost at water level as far as Mauzac. The Dordogne at this part appears to be a wide, shallow river with wide gravel banks in midstream, and reeds and bushes floating close to the surface of the water. This is, in fact, something of an artificial illusion for the height of the stream, here and elsewhere, is controlled by a series of dams and barrages and the water diverted for use in the production of hydro-electricity. One such barrage with huge iron sluices spans the river at Mauzac. Behind the barrage the river rises by about 20 feet and becomes instantly a slow, grave stream. Below the barrage, notices along the banks warn the public of dangers of camping on the islands mid-stream, or wading out to fish. The operation of the sluices can make a rapid difference to the level of the water and cause the unsuspecting angler or camper quite an unpleasant surprise. Not far from Mauzac, on the south bank, lies the fine old castle of Badefols. Unlike most of the castles, Badefols is in ruins with great trees growing within the walls, and their green leaves flowing over the walls, giving the castle a surprised look, like an old man with bright

101

View of the Dordogne from the Cingle de Trémolat

green hair. At Badefols the river begins the great sweep known as the Cingle de Tremolat.

These *Cingles*, or bends, are caused by harder levels in the limestone forcing the river away from its natural course until it forms a great loop. The effect, from above, for example from the viewpoint by the Hôtel Panorama, is wonderful. The cliff drops down to the river far below, where on either side, in front of the spectator, the river sweeps round the opposite point, two great arms enclosing a green hill, while across the water bridges march at intervals down the river like steps in a ladder. The *Cingle* at Tremolat is particularly beautiful, and the views over the *Cingle* from the north bank bring people from miles to admire the sights.

Tremolat itself, below the hill overlooking the *Cingle,* is a pleasant village, with a fine fortified church—and a massive place it is, without charm and with all the marks of a stronghold. Tremolat, thanks to the deepening of the river caused by the barrage lower down, has become a great centre for water sports with rowing, canoeing, sailing, and water-skiing all regular events in the summer months.

It is also a great cycling centre. Cycles can be hired in the village and the roads round about are full of cycle parties, usually family groups, with the smaller children seated behind their parents, on little panniers.

At Limeuil where the Vézère joins with the Dordogne, stands the beautiful Pont Coude, which spans both rivers at this point. Le Pont Coude means 'the elbow bridge', and that is exactly what it is, but how much better it sounds in French! Limeuil is an attractive town with curtain walls and a lot of medieval homes. The Dordogne is shallow again here, which gives some indication of how rapidly the land is rising, and flows fast over gravel banks. The southern road from Lalinde reaches the far side of Le Pont Coude and this route may appeal to those who do not want to face the climb up over the *Cingle*. It also gives excellent views of the limestone cliffs that contain the river in this section. If we cross the Pont Coude here, on to the south bank and turn east for Siorac, we can then continue past Siorac towards the castle country.

The first castle that looms up is at Berbiguières, which is challenged from the north bank by the château of Fage which tops the green slope on the far hill above St. Cyprien. This southern road

Le Pont-Coude—the Elbow Bridge

gives one wonderful views into the valley and over the river, and by veering down towards the river one comes on a block of castles, all different, and all picturesque.

To the first, Les Milandes the celebrated, exotic dancer, Miss Josephine Baker, once the toast of Paris, retired with her large family of adopted children. Set up among deep woods, and among beautiful gardens, it is a wonderful place for children, and would that more people put their retirement to such good use.

Not far from Les Milandes, just by the road, lies the lovely château of Fayrac. Fayrac was the home of Henry of Navarre's great captain, Geoffrey de Vivans, stormer of cities, and it glowers across the valley to the town and castle of Beynac on the far shore. Beynac is a splendid place, as befits a town that was, in its time, the centre of one of the four great baronies of Périgord. Beynac, too, was a Huguenot stronghold, and together with Fayrac they sealed

104

Feyrac

105

off the valley from the Catholic west. To get to Beynac, you drive along to the bridge at Castelnaud Fayrac, where the fine castle of Castelnaud stands, 1,000 feet above the valley on a great green hill. The castle was built in the twelfth century and changed hands several times in the Hundred Years War. The views over the valley from Castelnaud are fantastic.

Beynac was occupied, and held in fee, that is at the King's pleasure, by Mercadier, captain of Richard Coeur-de-Lion's *routiers*. The castle was largely rebuilt in the thirteenth century, and was one of the places where the *parlement* of Périgord met in the Middle Ages. The town of Beynac itself is full of fine medieval buildings and the climb up to the castle is, to say the least, invigorating, but the beautiful Hôtel Bonnet, by the river, would repay anyone for the effort.

Outside Beynac I had an eyeball to eyeball confrontation with a peacock. In my admittedly limited experience with peacocks, they are usually encountered strutting about in a superior fashion on the lawns of stately homes, periodically letting themselves down by emitting blood curdling screams. Imagine my surprise, therefore, to encounter one, not only by a small farmhouse, but actually perched in a tree beside the road, like any common bird. A peacock with tail displayed is a lovely sight, and, braking hurriedly, I emerged from the car with the camera. Alarmed, the peacock lowered its tail. When I got back in the car, the tail was again displayed. When I got out, down it went. This went on for some time. Then I thought of the sliding roof, through which, smiling craftily, I proceeded to emerge. As the camera was levelled, the bird, stunned at this manifestation of human guile, sprang to life, and letting out one of those paralysing yells, dived headlong out of the tree, and legged it into the barn. I shall never feel quite the same about peacocks after that.

Along the road from Beynac lies the riverside fortress of La Roque Gageac. Here, on the site of a medieval fortress similar in style and intention to the cliff dwellings of Tayac, a modern terrace of houses has been built in the style of medieval houses. If proof were needed of the attraction of pure style, fashioned in natural material, this is it. The houses rise and fall with the cliffs in a series of terraces connected with wide steps, and blend with the cliffs in a manner most pleasing to the eye. The site itself is an unlikely one, braced up hard under the cliffs, with only the road to separate it from the river. The river here is very popular with sunbathers, swimmers, and fishermen, for the gravel banks make perfect sun-traps. Many people seem to manage to both bathe and fish, wading into the river waist deep to cast their lines. The river gets put to good recreational use, and the camping sites along the banks, as we have noted before, are really wonderful. All seem to be placed at attractive spots, and even in the high season do not seem overcrowded.

La Roque Gageac has one of the many passenger ferries across the river that supplement the numerous bridges. This one is operated by a cable, and can take passengers across the river in record time.

At La Roque Gageac we turn north to Sarlat, the main town serving this part of the valley, and home of Michel de Montaigne's great friend Etienne de la Boetie.

Montaigne was twenty-five when he met la Boetie, and they formed instantly a friendship that endured until la Boetie's early death. Montaigne refers to la Boetie constantly in his Essays, and la Boetie was clearly one of the great, if not the only, human influence in his life. 'If you ask me why I love him,' he writes, 'I can only say, because it was he, because it was I.' La Boetie died in 1563 and Montaigne was desolate.

La Boetie was born in 1530 in a fine house, of the mid-fifteenth century, just opposite the cathedral, and has more claims to justify his memory than his friendship with Montaigne. As the Magistrate of Sarlat, he upheld the law in an unbiased fashion, and, although a devout Catholic, extended the protection of the law to Huguenots. He translated various works from the Greek, and made significant contributions to the common understanding of French political thought at that time. And when you consider the confusion of French political thought for his time, this is no mean achievement.

Sarlat, now the centre of the Sardalaise, was once the capital of the Périgord Noir. It is a tourist centre, a market town, and has a large artistic colony, some of whom display their wares outside the church of St. Sacerdos, as merchants and craftsmen must have done for a thousand years. The church of St. Sacerdos, one of those obscure saints after whom the French usually choose to name their cathedrals and great churches, was rebuilt in 1504, and is even

The house of La Boetie in Sarlat

now undergoing significant reconstruction. In the churchyard is another of the peculiar Lanterne des Morts, much larger than the one at Athur near Périgueux.

Local legend has it that this one was erected at the wish of St. Bernard of Clairvaux, who preached the First Crusade from this spot.

Lanternes des Morts are curious. No one seems to know why they were built, and no one feels certain enough to advance a positive theory. The one at Sarlat is certainly big enough to contain coffins, and, to suggest a theory, it might be that they were built to hold the bodies of plague victims or lepers, or strangers who died in or around the town and whose bodies had nowhere to rest while they awaited burial in consecrated ground. The light in the lanterne would keep people away from the area of infection. This is only a theory, and like everyone else, I have no real faith in it.

Sarlat gives one the feel of a medieval town. Like Périgueux, it has always been prosperous and large enough to live on its own wealth and industry and not need the present wealth of tourism. One day the world will wake up to the terrible cost it pays for inviting the other world into its home cities. A town that lives on tourism is debauched and it would not be too strong to say that in this day and age tourism has reached the point of being a pollution. I say this in full knowledge that this book will bring more tourists to the Dordogne, and I say it unrepentently. It is not the fact that the visitors come, that matters, it is that they should be allowed to come if they care to, and not to be cajoled by the creation of artificial attractions, or by the prostitution of ancient life and customs into a daily spectacle.

In the case of Sarlat, the visitor who takes the trouble to do so will get more feel of the Middle Ages during a quiet walk in the Cathedral, than from watching a full-scale medieval joust laid on by the local riding club and Syndicat d'Initiative.

Leaving Sarlat, and heading south towards the river again, brings one to the little village of Vitrac. Vitrac offers some splendid walks along the valley, and some fine fishing.

Five kilometres south of Vitrac, across the Dordogne, lies the fortress *bastide* of Domme. Domme is a dream. It is a perfect little town, beautiful at first sight, even more beautiful when being

Lanterne des Morts in Sarlat

visited, and explored. Anyone would wax lyrical about it and for beauty it beggars description. It stands, a jewel in golden stone, on a tall hill, overlooking a switchback, winding road, that heaves itself up through a just wide enough gateway and into the outer square of the town.

Domme is a *bastide*. The beauty of these foundations is so outstanding, especially when one remembers that they were built for war, that we can only wonder at the skill of the architect in creating something so fine. The town was built for Philip le Hardi, King of France, and has all the usual *bastide* features, but without the arcades. The town rises and falls over the hilltop, with straight streets and alleys all linking up the fortifications. In one of the towers, that of the Porte des Tours, the visitor can see the names and arms of the captive Knights Templar, many of whom were incarcerated here, after the Order was suppressed in the fourteenth century. The present inhabitants of Domme are clearly as impressed with the beauty of the place as is the summer visitor, for they have enhanced the charm of the town with pots and baskets of flowers, long window boxes, and neat gardens to provide bright splashes of colour against the golden stones.

From the heights of Domme, views over the river valley are naturally wonderful, and lunch on the terrace of the hotel there must be one of the most satisfying meals in the world, apart from the excellence of the menu. Mighty Domme, once the key to the southern *bastides*, is still conquering people who come within her walls, and being so beautiful it is really no wonder.

When Domme was built she was declared by Philip le Hardi to be impregnable. But then it was his words, rather than his actions, that gave him the nickname of 'the Bold'. In fact Domme like most other towns changed hands regularly in the Hundred Years War, and was refortified and supplied with cannon by the Catholics when the Wars of Religion swept over this part of France.

Domme then justified the faith of her creator for many years, in fact until the year 1588, which proved so decisive for Protestant affairs in Europe, with the English defeat of Spain's Great Armada. The Huguenot cause in the south-west had also been going well since Coutras, and Henry of Navarre's great captain, Geoffrey de Vivans, who had already taken Sarlat, moved against Domme. De Vivans had been born nearby at Fayrac, and therefore knew Domme

The gateway to Domme

112

well, including the reputation it had for being impregnable to assault. He was aware of the strength of the great curtain *bastide* walls, and, one would like to think, he hesitated before smashing such a beautiful town with his siege artillery. He decided therefore on a stratagem. At night, with a party of only thirty unarmoured men, he scaled the walls above the cliffs, rightly suspecting the walls would be deemed unscaleable and lightly guarded. Meanwhile, his army made a noisy demonstration before the gates, and under cover of the noise and confusion, De Vivans and his party entered the town, and overcame the watch.

Before the garrison knew what was happening, the main gate was in their hands, and the Huguenot cavalry were racing through the streets of the town.

De Vivans held the town for four years, until 1592, and established it as the centre of Protestant power in the middle Dordogne. When he finally left, having sold the town to the Catholics of Bordeaux, he marched out with all the honours of war, standards flying, drums beating, and matches lit, leaving behind a town undamaged in the wars, and very largely as we see it today.

Before leaving Domme, the traveller should go down and visit the Grotto du Jubile, in the limestone cliffs and nearby, the little monolithic chapel of Caudon, hewn out of the limestone rock, like the one at St. Emilion. This done, the traveller can continue his journey, on to the east and north.

113

CHAPTER IX

Along the Dordogne—Montfort to Beaulieu

After Domme, as we proceed up river, through more of the castle country, between Montfort and Beaulieu, the river changes. It is now very steady, compressed by the encroaching foothills of the Massif Central and more precisely by the Causse de Martel, one of the great plateaux that reach down from the central mountain range. During this section also, at Souillac, the river leaves Périgord, and enters Quercy turning north to its birthplace in the Massif Central.

The river remains charming, and the countryside is full of interesting sights. The scenery changes only in that it adds grandeur to spectacle. High, forested cliffs encage the river, as a foretaste of the mountains to come.

The most wonderful thing about the Dordogne country, apart from the weather and the absence of crowds, is the continual supply of beautiful sights, both man-made and natural. Every day the traveller will see something that he tells himself is unsurpassed so far, and unsurpassable, only to discover that day, or the next, something else, not better perhaps but as beautiful, and different.

Variety is the ingredient that prevents even beauty itself becoming monotonous. Louis XV's doctor once remarked, admittedly in a different context, that variety is the greatest aphrodisiac. He was, of course, a cynic, but the variety of the Dordogne is certainly the thing that makes the traveller fall in love with it. Hautefort, Brantôme, Bourdeilles, the *bastides*, Biron, and latterly Domme: all are wonderful, and none is remotely like the rest.

From Domme perched high on a hill on the south bank, we have to come down again, across the river at Vitrac, where there are some fine hotels, to the great castle of Montfort. Montfort is the classic castle of the Dordogne, the one that appears in all the posters, and on approaching it, one can see why. It is a large and beautiful place so secure and solid on the very verge of the sheer drop down to the river that one imagines it being built inland, on safer ground and then slid sideways into place.

Montfort perches on the cliff like an eagle, and from such an eyrie, can sweep the river valley for miles, as it passes below on the sweep of the Montfort *Cingle*.

Like the Cingle de Tremolat, that at Montfort sweeps north, with the castle at the apex of the curve.

Montfort has a long and warlike history. It was built in the twelfth century, and in 1214 was stormed and taken by Simon de Montfort, not the victor of Lewes and founder of the English Parliament, who died at Evesham, but his grandfather, also Simon, who led the Pope's army south against the heretics of Albi. He took the castle, and held it for his own, and began the first of many alterations and reconstructions.

On such a commanding site, it was the scene of much fighting during the Hundred Years War, and was captured by both French and English in their turn. During the Wars of Religion, it fell to the Huguenots. Every siege destroyed some part of the fabric, and every rebuilding added to the castle's beauty and variety. The castle we see today contains a mixture of every period from the twelfth to the sixteenth centuries, but is largely fifteenth century, and is still inhabited, part of the keep containing an excellent restaurant. The view from the walls is naturally superb and the castle attracts crowds of visitors in the summer months.

Near Montfort lies the pretty village of Carsac. There was an abbey there in the Middle Ages which is now the village church. This church has undergone the most careful reconstruction since the war, and the old medieval framework is now shown to best advantage.

The churchyard is a riot of wildlife, with vivid green lizards scampering over the stones, butterflies hovering among the grasses, and the usual clouds of swifts and swallows darting about the sky.

In an area as devoted to agriculture and field sports as the Dordogne, there is naturally an abundance of wildlife. Most noticeable to the casual traveller are the clouds of butterflies which flutter everywhere in the deep meadows and along the grassy banks

The chateau at Montfort

beside the roads. One frequently hears the economist lament the inefficiency of the French farmer, and the low level of productivity on their farms. If this is partly due to traditional methods of cultivation and the restricted use of chemical sprays, then the world at large has much to be grateful for, for these sprays have destroyed the British butterflies, which were once so common, until now to see any at all is a rare event on a country walk. In the Dordogne the lepidopterist would find himself in paradise, while the traveller can again enjoy the pleasures of sitting on a wall and watching beautiful butterflies flit aimlessly about. Birds, some familiar and others more exotic, are common, and the woods and fields are full of birdsong. Deer frequent the high Causse country and the smaller mammals, fox, weasel, squirrel, and rabbit are frequent sights sprinting across the road.

Domestic animals abound, sheep and cattle in the meadows, horses for work and recreation, while every farm has bright brown hens pecking happily around the yard, and a scurry of rabbits from hutches along the wall of the barn.

The great domestic bird of the Dordogne is, of course, the goose. Doomed to be fed to death, they march in large companies around the fields in their flocks with a gaggle of goslings hard behind, elbowing each other out of the way in the effort to keep up with mother. They seem surprisingly unferocious.

When I was a boy I spent my holidays on the farm of my aunt in Wiltshire. My aunt, who was eccentric to a degree, kept a variety of pets, including a sheep and Manx cats, and a large gander. This bird delighted in chasing me round the farm, neck outstretched, hissing loudly, whenever I had just arrived from school. By the end of the holiday, we would be firm friends, and it would accompany me everywhere, peering myopically at anything I happened to discover. Regretfully though, it had a very short memory, and would be as unfriendly as before when I next came to stay. From these early encounters, I have always viewed geese with a degree of circumspection. Neither am I particularly fond of goats, which are a common sight in the Dordogne, where their milk makes the delicious *fromage de chèvre*.

Which brings us directly to food.

In a land like the Dordogne, with so much to offer, I must confess to finding the food a disappointment. This can only be coupled

117

with the fact that in French eyes, the cuisine of Périgord is one of the marvels of France. For myself I find the regional dishes are over-rated and of limited appeal. Dishes cooked *a la Périgordienne* would be cooked in walnut oil, from all those walnut trees, and flavoured or garnished with truffles, the so-called Black Gold of Périgord.

Truffles, as we have mentioned, live off young oaks, and can only be obtained fresh in November or December. The summer visitor is, therefore, not likely to meet a truffle face to face, in a state of nature, as it were, which may well prove a blessing in disguise. The truffle is a wonderful catalyst for enhancing the flavour of an omelette or pâté, but on its own the truffle has the appearance and consistency of coke. It makes up for its indifferent appearance by a most pungent and penetrating aroma, which is not so much unpleasant as unavoidable. A small truffle, purchased at vast cost, and placed for safe keeping in the glove compartment, had, within twelve hours, made the car uninhabitable. One of us had to go, and the truffle went into a nearby stream. Truffles do not make good pets, but as an ingredient to improve some other dish they are delightful.

Omelettes made from the fresh eggs of those farmyard fowls are always good value, while the local *omelette aux cèpes*, made with a variety of wild mushroom, is a feast which, with a good local pâté or terraine (which once made should be kept for a few months to mature), and taken with a glass of Bergerac or Monbazillac, makes a perfect lunch.

Other specialities of the region include duck, guinea fowl, hare and, of course, the goose, prepared in various ways and usually garnished with truffles. Fish, especially trout and salmon, appear on most menus and are well prepared. The great joy of the area, for the visitor, is the fruit. Peaches, cherries, apples, and pears grow here in profusion, and freshly picked and juicy, make a perfect end to a meal. Strawberries are another local delicacy, and Vergt in Dordogne is the strawberry capital of France.

The strawberries are usually marinated for a few hours before serving, in a dish of claret and sugar. This brings out the flavour of the fruit most effectively.

The local liqueurs also come from local produce. Two regularly offered as *digestifs* are the *eau de vie de prunes*, and the *eau de noix*, this last a speciality of Martel, in the Causse.

Like most Englishmen, I view anything to do with prunes with decided suspicion but it can be sampled in *dégustation* centres, and once tried, is found to be not at all unpalatable.

It will be seen, therefore, that in spite of my opening remarks, the cuisine of Périgord is of great variety, and any gourmet who makes the journey there will have no cause to lament the trip.

But let us now leave the subject of good living and proceed on our journey.

Crossing the river east of Montfort, and turning towards Veyrignac, brings one to the fine castle at Fénelon, which offers the visitor spectacular views over the river, north towards Ponfillac. Fénelon has great curtain walls, dating from the fifteenth century, and some fine towers, but is chiefly noted as the birthplace of the writer François de Salignac, who was born here in 1651 and in later life, at Carenac, wrote extensively under the name of Fénelon.

Over the river again, and blessing the abundance of bridges, we go through Rouffillac, and along the north bank towards Souillac.

The Causse de Gramat comes sweeping down to the river here, and a quiet, bare wall of white limestone overlooks the valley as we come into Souillac from the west. The river here is again wide and shallow, dotted with the odd small island and with plenty of fine 'campings' in evidence along the banks. On the grass of one camping, outside Souillac, lay a great fleet of canoes, which proved to be carrying a party of Swiss canoeists down to Bordeaux from Argentat. Above Argentat the river is controlled by high dams, but below, it makes a perfect path for canoeists, for their draught alone can cope with the shallow and the rough water. This party, typical of many that descend the Dordogne in the summer, was having a fine time, paddling gaily down in the day, and staying at a different 'camping' every night.

Entering Souillac, we have moved out of Périgord and into the nearby province of Quercy. Souillac is a fine town, the largest in this region of the Dordogne, and dominated by yet another of those domed and minareted churches of the Périgordian-Romanesque which we first encountered at Périgueux.

The cupolas look quite out of place around the other medieval buildings of the French south-west, giving as they do, a Byzantine air to the church. This is probably where the style came from, for many men from the town and district went on the First Crusade, and undoubtedly returned impressed with the buildings of Constantinople, then, and for 300 years afterwards, the greatest city in the known world. While my appetite for church architecture is easily blunted, the great church of Souillac is well worth inspection.

The cathedral at Souillac

Perhaps the men of Souillac erected the church to remind them of the time when they were young, and fighting the Infidel in Outremer. Whatever the reason this church and others like it are remarkable sights. The one at Souillac was, like many of these large south-western churches, once an Abbey, and is now the church of Ste. Marie. The tympanum over the west door relates the cautionary tale of Brother Theophile. He badly wanted to build the church and the

Devil, who feels very much at home in these old Angevin lands, heard his prayer and offered to help him build one, at the price of his soul. Luckily, when the time came for the monk to pay up, the Virgin intervened and saved him from his unpleasant fate. These carvings are well worth seeing, for they are extremely clear and rather disturbing.

Overlooking the square stands the clock-tower of the church of St. Eloi, which is a landmark when seen from the surrounding hills and it overlooks the entire town.

The English burnt the town during the Hundred Years War, while in 1562 it suffered the fate of Domme and Sarlat, and fell to the Huguenots, who made it a centre for the Protestant religion. Nowadays it makes a good centre for exploring the middle river or the Causses, and the Hôtel la Renaissance or the Hôtel Périgord are both very comfortable, with good menus which include local dishes.

Following the course of the increasingly winding river, we come to the picturesque seventeenth century castle at La Treyne, which, seen from the bridge over the river flowing swiftly below the walls, is a fine sight. Here the river contains submerged tree trunks and great branches, relics of the winter rains. West of La Treyne where the Dordogne is joined by a tributary river, the Ouisse, the aptly named Belcastel stands on a cliff over the river. This really is the beautiful castle, and not even Montfort is as well situated, with the blue river winding below the sheer white cliff, with the green valley and hills cupping the castle on every side. Belcastel was largely reconstructed in the last century and from the terraces below the towers wonderful views can be obtained over the valley, far into the distance.

To the east of Belcastel in a region of subterranean caves and grottoes, lies one of the great natural wonders of France, the great grotto and underground river at Padirac. This is one of the sights that the visitor to the region must not miss, and if, as is by no means impossible, the family has lost their appetite for castles and churches, then a visit to Padirac will be a refreshing change. Such a stop has long been a popular visit, and over the years a considerable tourist complex has grown up around the grotto. There is, for example, a zoo, a bird park, several restaurants, and some nice bars. In the sunshine it all looks very pleasant and relaxed, and

The Chateau La Trayne

122

those who do not relish a trip to the bowels of the earth will find plenty to entertain them until the family returns.

The great hole of Padirac was once thought to be a gateway to hell, and it was not until 1889 that the underground river, below the hole, was discovered. Over the next ten years expeditions pushed deeper and deeper into the caves, and in 1947, by introducing a coloured dye into the water, it was confirmed that the waters eventually flow into the Dordogne near Montvalent over five miles away. The cavern itself, which is huge, was created by the action of rivers under the Causse de Gramat, until they eventually forced a way through the soft sub-strata, to the main river. The action of the water has created great stalactites and stalagmites, and a number of waterfalls which prevent the river being navigable for the entire length. To visit the cavern the traveller descends some 300 feet, by a series of lifts. Padirac is very large, without the oppressive closeness of the Grand Roc at Les Eyzies and no one who feels fine on the London underground will be distressed at Padirac. It would be well, though, to take an anorak or raincoat for, be it never so hot above, down below it strikes chill, with a steady rain of drips falling from the cavern roof far above. Once below, you proceed along well lit passages to the embarkation point for a cruise along the river. The trip is taken in flat-bottomed punts poled by guides in the manner of Venetian gondoliers, who keep up a continual patter of information as you go.

The water is crystal clear, and where it is too deep the poling is off the walls, for the river passage, though often high, is never very wide. After almost a mile you alight at a small jetty where the guides take you on a tour of the waterfalls and the great cavern, which you ascend in a series of steps before returning to your boat again. The total trip takes about an hour and is a definite experience, one not to be missed. Back on the surface we turn after the Dordogne again, north, to visit the beautiful abbey at Carenac. The village of Carenac has some fine medieval houses, and is the centre for the production of the potent *eau de prune*, but is historically famous for its connections with the writer François de Salignac, or Fénelon.

Within the abbey walls of Carenac, Fénelon wrote some of the great classic works of the French language, notably his *Télémaque*. Fénelon was Prior of the abbey and the little island in the Dordogne

A bust of Fénelon

opposite the walls is popularly supposed to be the 'Isle de Calypso' featured in his work. In all events it is pointed out as such to the visitor, and one should not doubt a good story. Carenac was a Cluniac foundation, and dates from 1050. When the abbey was suppressed in 1788, only four monks still lived there.

Along the river now, to Bretenoux, where the Dordogne is joined by yet another of her many tributary rivers, the Céré running in from the east. The Dordogne changes direction here, and to stay

The red castle at Castelnau

with her we must do likewise and head north past the great red walls of the castle at Castelnau.

Castelnau is a fine château, very old, with parts dating back to the ninth century, and in its hey-day, during the Middle Ages, was a major garrison, housing many archers and men at arms.

125

We go north, on the west bank, to our last port of call on the river: the historic and beautiful town of Beaulieu.

Standing at the meeting point of the three provinces of Périgord, Quercy and Limousin, Beaulieu is an old town, where the Benedictine abbey, like the castle at Castelnau, dates back to the ninth century. The west door is intricately carved with scenes from the Day of Judgement, and the whole building is very striking.

Canoeists on the Dordogne near Beaulieu

Nearly overlooking the river is the Penitents' Chapel, another fine building although, like the church, in need of some restoration.

Beaulieu itself, the 'beautiful place' is the last river town we shall visit. From here the road runs up to Argentat, above which the river is so much in the grip of hydro-electric schemes that the nature of the stream has totally changed.

Anyone who enjoys vast sweeps of water, and the walls of dams, will find the road above Argentat very interesting, but along the twelve miles from Beaulieu to Argentat lies some of the most beautiful scenery in the Dordogne valley. We can follow this road up to Argentat, and then head west through the Causse to the busy little town of Brive-La-Gaillarde.

Here, in the Place Winston Churchill, are a selection of hotels, where we can plan the final stage of our journey, a trip down the Causse country.

CHAPTER X

The Causse Country

Not everyone likes rivers. The river country has many admirers and a wide choice of delights, but those who crave the high plateau and the windswept, open fields can find a complete and invigorating change of scene in the Causse country.

The word 'Causse' means plateau, and, these great Causses lie, like steps in a ladder, astride the Dordogne river, and to the east of the Department. They are from the north, the Causse de Martel, the Causse de Gramat, and, below Cahors, the Causse de Limoges.

The Causses are a result of the upheaval that created the Massif Central, and the action of the rivers, making their way down through the rock, cutting deep valleys out of the river bed. The Causses are best imagined as the fingers projecting from a clenched fist, where the knuckles are the central spine of the Massif. When the Massif arose, in primeval times, it tilted the whole of the land sideways, to the west, and the rivers that now rise in the Massif run south-west to the Atlantic. As we have mentioned before, the line level of the land is on the Causse. We go down to the river rather than up to the plateau, and although the rivers, as we have seen, have created much natural beauty as they carved their way down to the valley floor, they have left a lot behind them on the heights.

The limestone of the Causses is porous; there are few streams. The water soaks into the rock and collects into underground lakes which in time force their way out, forming underground rivers and grottoes, like the one at Le Grand Roc, and the one we have already visited at Padirac.

Lacking water, the Causse is a dry, bare country. The bones of the land lie close to the surface of the earth, breaking through in places to lie in strips, like grey ribs, on the surface of the fields. Every rain washes rocks to the surface and these have been pain-fully collected off the fields and built into drystone walls that edge the farmland. Agriculture, usually sheep or arable farming, continues to dominate the region and the usual walnut trees, a little smaller now, still grow on the scanty earth.

Up on the Causse, the traveller looks down across the deep blue-green valleys to the rivers far below, and the tall limestone cliffs rearing up from the forests on either side. It is spectacular country; the roads across it swoop up and down, and around and over, surging about as they gain height on the one hand and lose it again on the other.

From the north the traveller can swoop on the Causse country from Brive-la-Gaillarde, an underrated little town, better known as a stop on the road to Spain than an attraction in its own right. Heading south from Brive, climbing steadily up the smoother north face of the Causse de Martel, the traveller soon espies across the valley the crowded hilltops of Turenne, where the Tower of César on the castle prods an index finger at the sky. Turenne reeks of war and gave its name and title to that great French soldier Louis XIV's Marshal, the Vicomte de Turenne.

Henry de la Tour d'Auvergne, the first great soldier of the family, was a captain of Henry of Navarre, and commanded the Huguenot forces in the Limousin. It was his grandson, another Henry, that worked wonders in Flanders for Louis XIV winning battle after battle in the War of Devolution. Honours and wealth were heaped upon him, and he left a fortune in gold and honour to his family when he was buried at St. Denis, among the kings and heirs of France.

From this high point the fortunes of the family disappeared, and in the next century they were forced to sell their lands at Turenne to the crown; they were bought by Louis XV for over £4 million.

One of the sprigs of this house, Nicolas, fought a famous duel at the Rond Pont du Champs-Elysées with the notorious rake, Giacomo Casanova, and somewhat to his surprise, lost, receiving a thrust in the thigh. He might have guessed that anyone with Casanova's gift for outraging husbands would need to be deft with a rapier.

The castle and town of Turenne date from the sixteenth century, and present excellent examples of the buildings, noble and humble, of the period. The Tower of César is older than the rest of the castle and dates from the thirteenth century. Needless to say, it has nothing to do with the great Julius but many great buildings of the Middle Ages were given some lordly title and anything as outstanding as Turenne's great tower justifies a noble name.

South of Turenne, across the Causse, lies Martel from which the Causse takes its name. Martel is a magnificent little town, steeped in history. The town is named after the great Charles Martel, who, after defeating the Saracens at Poitiers in AD 732, pursued their army south and finally broke them up near the spot on which Martel now stands. Charles founded the church of St. Maur to commemorate the victory. The word Martel means hammer, and the arms of Charles Martel with three hammers are shown in relief over one of the doors to his church. St. Maur is a fine building set deep in the town, surrounded, as in medieval time, with cobbled courtyards and alleys. The tympanum over the main door is particularly striking showing Christ in glory, surrounded by angels with trumpets. Inside, the church retains much of the medieval wall painting, and is well worth inspecting. Nearby is the Hôtel de la Raymondie built in the thirteenth century by the Turenne family and now the town hall and tourist office. At the tourist office I had some discussion concerning the correct naming of Henry II of England's eldest son, also Henry, whom the French and some English, persist in calling Henry 'Curt-Mantel'. This, while enabling us to tell the two Henrys apart, is quite incorrect. The story is somewhat complicated, as is much of the history of that remarkable and violent family.

Henry II, called Plantagenet, Count of Anjou, was not King of England when he married Eleanor of Aquitaine.

Stephen of Blois still ruled England, but he died shortly after Henry and Eleanor were married, and the couple rode north to claim this addition to their already extensive lands. Fresh from his nuptials, Henry arrived in England wearing new clothes, including a then fashionable item, a short cape that hung from his shoulders to his waist.

His English nobles, who wore the long, floor-length cloaks so necessary in their draughty northern castles, were much amused at this impractical southern garment, and nicknamed Henry, 'Curt-Mantel'—'short cloak'. This name was in common use years before the Young Henry was even born. In the idiom of the time he should correctly be called Henry Fitz Henry, but in 1170 his father Henry

Martel

131

II, seeking to ensure the peaceful succession for his House, had his son crowned and made the nobles swear loyalty to him as their lord. This meant that the nobles were put in a difficult position when as eventually happened, the two Kings fell out. For, having sworn loyalty to both Kings, which should their nobles follow in battle? Moreover, how to differentiate between the two King Henrys. The people at the line called him simply the Old King and the Young King, and where or when subsequent generations transferred the Old King's nickname to his son, I cannot discover.

I explained the difficulty and this story to the lady at the Syndicat d'Initiative. She took me out to the street and pointed out the sign reading *Rue de Henri Curt-Mantel*. That to her seemed to settle the matter for the sign was on the wall of the Maison Fabbri where Henry, the Young King, died in agony and remorse after sacking the shrine at Rocamadour in 1183. Martel is also the centre for the manufacture of the *eau de noix*, mentioned in the previous chapter, which can be sampled at various parts in the town, and one can tour the ramparts and the seven *tours* the town is noted for, and take a little refreshment gratis while doing so.

The *dégustation*, or tasting shops, are most generous with their samples, and it often takes considerable resistance and self control to avoid having too much. The method is shrewd though, for even those who go in only to taste usually come out with a bottle. Like the *eau de prunes*, *eau de noix* is an acquired taste, but very palatable.

From Martel it is only a short distance, across the Dordogne and through Montvalet, to the spectacular pilgrimage site of Rocamadour, on the Causse de Gramat. Rocamadour lies in the deep valley of the river Alzou, and the first sight of the little town, clinging to the cliff face in the far side of the ravine is enough to take the breath away. Rocamadour is, by repute, the second most beautiful town in France, and it is hard to think of the place that precedes it.

The town is situated on one side of a gigantic ravine, and, seen from across the void the town seems to hang in mid-air, unsupported. It is reached by climbing down, through a tunnel, out round the head of the valley and down again to the town. The visitor enters through the fortified main gate, and is at once in a medieval city. On either hand are the shops and stalls of tradesmen, while up

View of Rocamadour

133

on the right, tower the walls of the pilgrimage church. From the bottom runs the Staircase of the King, up which the pilgrims would climb painfully on their knees to reach the shrine of the Virgin, each holding a candle to burn at the shrine. Candles are still on sale at the foot of the staircase, and it may be that some pilgrim still comes to Rocamadour and feels that only the old ways will attract the attention and compassion of the Virgin.

Up the stairs past a little museum and a number of churches and chapels, lies the object of all this veneration, the Virgin of Notre Dame de Rocamadour, in her dark chapel.

Few places can still retain such a timeless air as this little chapel. The visitor enters a little blinded by the bright sunlight, and sees before him in their holders the ranks of the tall, white, smoking candles. The ceiling above is caked black with the soot from centuries of candle smoke, and high up are the chains and manacles of prisoners, who prayed for their release and brought their fetters to Rocamadour when they obtained it. Other, more recent, trinkets adorn the walls, for Rocamadour is no empty shrine. Pilgrims still come and sometimes, if their prayers are answered, they bring mementoes as an encouragement to others. Swords, ship-models, medals, and insignia of honour hang in their places around the walls, while from her niche in the corner the Virgin watches the door with an engaging gaze. This is a Black Virgin, blackened by time and immeasurably old, carved by some ancient craftsman. She is probably about 800 years old, and in her time has seen emperors and kings, saints, and a good many unrepented sinners kneel at her feet.

The Virgin at Rocamadour, as we have indicated, has always had a special sympathy for soldiers. In the Middle Ages knights called here to pray for her assistance in the fulfilling of some particular vow. Her shrine in those days was full of shattered lances, swords, and armour, all the trappings of war. Legend has it that Roland, who rode through here on his way to fight the Saracens at Roncesvalles, pledged that his sword Durandal should be placed there after his death, and so it was. Unfortunately, Roland was killed centuries before the grave of St. Amadour was discovered, but his sword at least, eventually, found its way there.

It was the Virgin's reputation as a friend of soldiers that brought her greatest disaster, when in 1183, Henry the Young King, in rebellion as usual against his father, rode down on Rocamadour and stole the treasure of the Virgin to pay his *routiers*. He even took Roland's sword, and rode off north with it hanging by his side. This was an act of sacrilege, and writs of anathema and excommunication would surely have caught up with the Young King, had not a more final fate overtaken him. Only a few miles away from the shrine, he was struck with a sudden illness, and, unable to ride, he was taken to Martel and lodged in the Maison Fabbri.

There, a few days later, he died. Of all his following only one man, the knight William the Marshal, remained with him, and the Young King died lying in the ashes on the floor of his lodging.

When the Young King sacked it, Rocamadour was already one of the great shrines of Europe, ranking with Santiago de Compostella and immensely rich. Curiously there was no great event or miracle to start the cult which brought the pilgrims. Some time in the eleventh century, some monks excavating for a cell, discovered a coffined body. It may have been that of an early anchorite monk, but the monks who discovered it declared it to be the body of Zaccharias a follower of Christ, and friend of Mary. The trickle of visitors soon grew to a flood, and the shrine of Amadour, the friend of Mary, was established. It was probably one of those early pilgrims that brought the statue of the Virgin, about which miracles were soon reported.

Modern man finds the idea of the pilgrimage and the veneration of relics evidence of the rather foolish attitude that our simpler forefathers had to the after-life. Living in a well-travelled world we know that there are enough pieces of the True Cross to build Noah's Ark and enough pieces of Noah's Ark to build enough ships to save all the inhabitants of Sodom and Gomorrah. Medieval man had no such information to undermine his faith, and he had faith also in the beneficial effects of the pilgrimage, and the veneration of relics in this life and in Heaven afterwards.

In this, the common man took his tone from the great princes, for no king's treasure was complete without a comprehensive stock of relics. These relics, or the 'halidom' as it was called, proved the king's piety, gave him something to turn to in hours of need, and came in handy for the swearing of powerful oaths. All Englishmen remember how Earl Harold was tricked by William of Normandy into swearing to support his claim to England on a box of holy

Pont Valentre at Cahors

relics. Relics were widely collected, and it is recorded that when Fulk Nerra, Count of Anjou, who had led a life of quite surpassing wickedness, went to Jerusalem to pray for forgiveness, he was so keen to obtain a piece of the Holy Shrine for his halidom that he bit a chunk off with his teeth.

The Virgin of Rocamadour is a curious relic of a simpler age, and few people can visit her chapel and not wonder at the power she has exerted on Christian pilgrims for centuries.

Rocamadour, which lies in the Department of the Lot, is today a centre for tourism, and almost totally commercialised. Tourists are, after all, the pilgrims of the twentieth century, and they probably, on balance, bring more blessings than they receive. They certainly throng the streets of Rocamadour and spend heavily before pouring back through the main gate to climb into their coaches and depart. Those who stay will enjoy the Hôtel de Ascensaur, or the Lion d'Or.

Rocamadour lies in a great fissure of the second Causse, the Causse de Gramat, which lies between the Dordogne and her southern sister the river Lot. Heading out of Rocamadour to the south, we pass over the high plateau of the Causse, and on to the little town with a name like a trumpet call, Labastide Murat.

Joaquim Murat was one of the twenty-six Marshals created by Napoleon, and the finest leader of light cavalry the world has ever seen. Dressed in the gorgeous uniforms of his own design, Murat led charges that smashed the armies of Europe from the path of the Emperor. There is a museum in the town which commemorates the exploits of this hero.

Murat's parents kept an inn in the town, and were disappointed when their son joined the army in 1788. Serving in Napoleon's brilliant campaigns in Italy, Murat soon distinguished himself and went on the expedition to Egypt; a few years later he married Napoleon's sister, Caroline. His advance was thereafter rapid and he eventually became, under Bonapartist patronage, the King of Naples. After the defeat at Waterloo, however, his decline was as rapid as his rise. He was driven from Naples by the returning Bourbons, and in attempting to recapture his kingdom, he was taken prisoner and shot.

Labastide Murat lies in the centre of the Causse de Gramat, which ends on the banks of the Lot. South again then, down the

137

Wall paintings at Rocamadour

valley of the river Vers which has cut itself a deep fissure in the Causse, until we emerge at Notre Dame de Velles, on the banks of the wide Lot itself, and turn towards Cahors. Throughout our tour of the Dordogne, Cahors has featured on every signpost, sometimes near and sometimes further away, but always there and serving now as the finishing point for our trip through the rivers and hills of the Dordogne. Cahors is not to be explored this time, but there is one sight still to be seen, and on the hill above it we can make an end. The Pont Valentre, a beautiful towered bridge, spans the Lot and takes the road south and out of this book. Across the Pont Valentre travelled the people who have inhabited these pages, and this is a good spot to say goodbye to them.

Samuel Johnson once remarked that any man who went to bed before midnight was a scoundrel. Any travel writer who can get to bed before midnight must be a genius. The preparation for his trip can occupy months before the high part of travelling the area actually starts, and when it does the work has not then really begun.

Maps must be studied, of varying size and scale, for there are routes to be plotted and time allocated. The country must be studied in depth, and the various, often conflicting, stories checked and reconciled. It is almost a relief to put all this behind one, in the boot of the car, and set off. Loaded like a pack-horse, with at least two cameras, tape-recorder, and notebooks, you plod heavily around the church and castle, old town and modern supermarket. Hoteliers and restaurateurs peer curiously at the scribbling figure in the corner, and people of all ages stare in wonder at the man talking to himself in the village square.

The writer must be incessantly curious. Anyone willing to talk must be talked to, and their comments carefully recorded, and in the evening after dinner the writer returns to his room and contemplates with increasing gloom the spools of tape, the rolls of film, and the pages of notes written in what now seems an indecipherable scrawl.

Out of all this, hopefully, will come a guide and story that others will enjoy and in that hope, I say 'bon voyage' and write

finis

Index

141

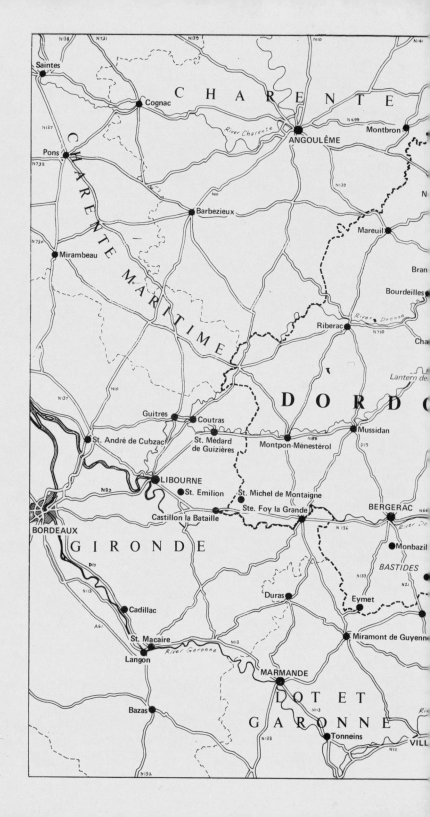